LEARNER'S POCKET

Word Skills

....

Ruth Gairns and
Stuart Redman

OXFORD
UNIVERSITY PRESS

OXFORD
UNIVERSITY PRESS

Great Clarendon Street, Oxford, OX2 6DP, United Kingdom

Oxford University Press is a department of the University of Oxford. It furthers the University's objective of excellence in research, scholarship, and education by publishing worldwide. Oxford is a registered trade mark of Oxford University Press in the UK and in certain other countries

ISBN: 978 0 19 462015 4   Student's Book
ISBN: 978 0 19 462016 1   Cover Card

Printed in China

This book is printed on paper from certified and well-managed sources

Cover by Carol Verbyst/NB Illustration Ltd

Contents

CONTENTS

Communication technology

Basic science

Dramatic events

C Everyday Topics

Food

CONTENTS

D Free Time

Holidays and travel

The arts

Sport

E Study and Work

Education

CONTENTS

Writing in English

Written exam questions

Work

Business and finance

F Society

Politics

The media

Crime

G Aspects of Language

Spoken English

Word formation

CONTENTS

Introduction

Oxford Learner's Pocket Word Skills can help you to increase your vocabulary in one compact, easy-to-use book.

There are 181 two-page units. These are divided into 31 modules, with each module covering different aspects of an important topic. For example, the module on 'Relationships' includes units on Friendship, Neighbours, Being a parent and Family history.

Each unit in a module presents and explains approximately 20 items of vocabulary. Some items are presented through pictures, e.g. types of vegetable or items of clothing, but more often the vocabulary is presented in different types of text so that you can see new words and phrases being used naturally. All the new vocabulary is shown in bold print.

After each text, a glossary explains the new vocabulary, and gives further important information to help you. This may be about grammar:

graffiti PL N drawings or writing on a wall, etc. in a public place.

trap sb OFTEN PASSIVE keep sb in a dangerous place or bad situation that they want to get away from but cannot.

There is also information about style:

> do a roaring trade INF sell a lot of sth
> very quickly.

> reactionary DISAPPROVING not wanting
> political or social change.

There are related words such as synonyms
or opposites:

> compulsory if sth is compulsory, you have
> to do it. SYN obligatory. OPP optional.

There are words from the same word
family:

> survive continue to live or exist despite
> being in a dangerous situation. survival N.

There are common word partners:

> conduct sth FML organize and do a
> particular activity: conduct an experiment

More information about a word or group
of words is often included in a word focus:

WORD FOCUS

Music on CDs, records and downloads
is produced as a **single** (= one song)
or an **album** (= a collection of songs).
One song on an album is called a **track**.

A wordlist is available on the website at
www.oup.com/wordskills which includes
all the words explained in this book. You
can use it as a reference for studying or to
test yourself.

An important feature of the book is the red cover card. This has been designed so that when the card is placed over a table or glossary, the words in red cannot be seen. This means you can test yourself on the new vocabulary: read the definitions and try to remember the word or phrase that is being defined. Do this as many times as you need – until you are sure that you have learnt it.

This book can be used alongside any English course. It includes most of the topics commonly found in course books, but teaches a range of vocabulary that course books do not have space for. There are more than 3,500 words and phrases taught in the book, corresponding to CEF levels B1-C2, with a particular emphasis on levels B2 and C1. This makes it ideal for learners who are preparing for IELTS, *Cambridge English*: *First* or *Cambridge English*: *Advanced*.

Facial appearance

1 wavy hair ▼ (see 11 and 16)
2 eyebrow
3 stubble
4 bald ADJ
5 beard
6 moustache
7 scar
8 His hair is receding/He's losing his hair/ He's going bald.
9 wrinkles He has wrinkles round his eyes.
10 clean-shaven (= with no beard or stubble).
11 curly hair
12 shoulder-length hair
13 freckles
14 This hairstyle is a bob.
15 fringe
16 straight hair
17 parting (You can have a centre parting as shown, or a side parting.)
18 tattoo
19 pierced ears
20 ponytail

WORD FOCUS

You can describe hair length: long, short, **shoulder-length, cropped** (= cut very short); also the thickness of the hair: **thick** (see picture 1) OPP **thin**. Hair is also described in terms of shape: **straight, curly, wavy**, also **frizzy** (= very curly) and **spiky** (= sticking straight up from your head).

Body shapes

She's slim.	thin in an attractive way.	Mostly used about girls or women.
a slender figure ▼	thin in an attractive or graceful way.	Mostly used about girls or women.
a skinny child	INF too thin and therefore not attractive.	This word is usually disapproving.
a lean, fit man	without fat; thin and fit.	Mostly used about men. Usually approving.
a plump little boy	a little fat in an attractive way, with a soft, round body/part of the body.	This is a more polite word than 'fat'.
a chubby baby	a little fat in a pleasant way.	Mostly used to describe babies and children.
a chubby face		
muscular arms	having large, strong muscles.	Used approvingly, mostly about men.
He's well-built.	big, with a strong, solid body.	Mostly used to describe men.
He's stocky.	short, with a strong, solid body.	Mostly used to describe men.

He's overweight.	too heavy and fat; weighing more than you should.	This is less rude than 'fat'. OPP underweight.
They're obese.	extremely fat in a way that is dangerous to someone's health. obesity N.	Obese is a medical term, but is also used in everyday English.
He's very lanky.	tall and with long, thin arms and legs, and not moving in an easy and graceful way.	Mostly used to describe teenage boys.
She's willowy.	tall, thin and graceful.	Mostly used to describe women.
She's petite.	short and attractively thin.	Mostly used to describe girls or women.

WORD FOCUS

Figure describes someone's body shape, especially a woman's: *She has a good figure.*
Build describes the size and shape of someone's body, especially a man's: *He's medium build.*
Physique is an approving word for someone's build, especially a man's: *a muscular physique.*

Good posture

If you work at a desk, avoid **slouching**, and don't **get stuck** in one position for hours **on end**; it's bad for your **posture**. Change your position: don't **bend over** your work all the time, but **lean back** when you're reading through something. Sit up **straight** when you are typing.

When you're sitting at your chair, try to keep your shoulders straight. From time to time you should **stretch** your neck **muscles** and **relax** your shoulders. **Tilt** your chair forward so that your knees are lower than your hips.

Keep both feet **flat** on the floor, NOT pulled back under your chair. **Crossing your legs** will **twist** your **spine** and put pressure on your knees and hips. If your feet don't **reach** the floor, put them on a low stool.

Finally, make sure that your chair is **adjusted** to the right height so that your eyes are **level with** the screen.

slouch stand, sit or move in a lazy way
    with your shoulders bent forward.

get stuck become unable to move.

on end without stopping: *for hours/days
    on end.*

posture the way you hold your body when
    standing or sitting.

bend (over/down) move the top part of
    your body forwards and downwards.

lean (back/forward) bend or move your
    body from a vertical position.

straight not curved or at an angle.

stretch sth push a part of your body out
    straight: *stretch your arms.*

muscle a piece of body tissue that you
    relax or stretch to move your arms,
    legs, etc.

relax sth make your muscles or part
    of your body less tight and more
    comfortable.

tilt sth move sth so that one end of it is
    higher than the other end.

flat in a level, straight position.

cross your legs place one leg over the
    other.

twist sth bend sth in an unnatural way.

spine the row of bones down your back.
    SYN backbone.

reach sth be able to touch sth.

adjust sth move sth slightly so that it is
    more comfortable or in the correct place.

level with sth having the same height,
    position, etc. as sth else.

Fitness

HOW **FIT** ARE YOU?

DO YOU lead a **sedentary** life, **slumped** in a chair all day? If so, you could be seriously **out of shape** and **badly in need of** exercise. Use these symptoms to **identify** your level of **fitness**:

- you feel **out of breath** ▼ after walking up a **flight of stairs**
- you feel **exhausted**, weak or **shaky** after just a few minutes of hard exercise
- your heart continues to **beat** fast for ten minutes after exercise
- you have poor **muscle tone**: for example, your muscles feel soft
- you **have trouble** getting to sleep at night after you **exercise**, and feel **abnormally** tired the next day
- you feel tired and **run down** most of the time
- you get **cramp** in your side after a very short run

It's **time to** get started on an exercise programme! ■

WORD FOCUS

If you are **out of breath** after exercise, you have difficulty **breathing** (= taking air in and out of your lungs); you need to **get your breath back/catch your breath**.

fit physically strong and healthy. **fitness** N.

sedentary in which you spend a lot of time sitting down: *a sedentary job/lifestyle.*

slumped sitting in a position which is not straight or upright, often without moving.

out of shape not in good physical condition. (You need to **get (yourself) into shape.**)

badly very much (used for emphasis).

in need of sth requiring sth that is important for health or happiness.

identify sth recognize a problem, need, etc. and understand exactly what it is.

flight (of stairs) a series of steps between two levels.

exhausted very tired.

shaky feeling weak and perhaps shaking because you are tired, ill, etc. SYN **unsteady.**

beat (of a heart) make a regular sound or movement.

muscle tone the strength of your muscles.

have trouble doing sth find it difficult to do sth.

exercise do a physical activity in order to stay healthy. (**do/take**) **exercise** N.

abnormally in a way that is different from normal.

run down tired and easily becoming ill.

cramp a sudden pain you get in your muscles, often after a lot of exercise.

time to do sth the time when sth should happen.

Ways of moving

'We **went for a stroll** ▼ in the park yesterday and Sam **trod on** a piece of metal which went through her shoe. She was **hopping about** and screaming in pain, and had to **limp** ▼ back home.'

'It was typical. Archie **marched** on ahead, leaving poor Lina and the kids **wandering** ▼ along behind him.'

'I watched the man **climb out of** the window, but then he **stumbled** and fell over, hitting his head. He started **crawling** along the path to the gate and eventually **got to his feet**. However, he was still **in a daze**, **staggering** slightly as if he was drunk.'

'I was **jogging** ▼ in the woods when this young guy **dashed** ▼ past me, **leapt** over a fallen tree and **ran off** into the distance. He was being **chased** by two policemen, but they were miles behind him.'

WORD FOCUS

Many verbs describing movement can also be used as nouns. Notice the verbs which go with these nouns.
Shall we go for a stroll?
She walks with a limp.
We had a wander round the town.
She goes for a jog every morning.
I made a dash for the exit.

stroll a slow, relaxed walk: *go for a stroll.*
  stroll v.

tread on/in sth put your foot down on or in sth while you are stepping or walking.

hop about move around by jumping on one foot.

limp walk slowly or with difficulty because one leg or foot is injured.

march 1 walk somewhere in a determined way (see text). **2** (of groups of people, especially soldiers) walk with stiff, regular steps at the same speed.

wander walk slowly around or to a place, without a particular direction or purpose.

climb out of sth get out of somewhere, especially with effort.

stumble hit your foot against sth while you are moving and fall over, or almost fall over.

crawl move forwards on your hands and knees.

get to your feet stand up.

in a daze unable to think clearly.

stagger walk or move with difficulty as if you are going to fall over.

jog run at a slow or steady speed for exercise or pleasure. jogging N.

dash go somewhere very quickly.

leap jump high or a long way.

run off suddenly leave a place or person.

chase sb/sth run or drive after sb in order to catch them. SYN pursue sb/sth FML.

Hearing

'I'm a drummer, so I've always **been exposed to** loud noise, but I've just discovered I'm **going deaf** ▼. My **hearing** isn't so bad in one ear, but I'm **partially deaf** ▼ in the other. I now have to listen to music **at full blast** or I can't hear the **lyrics**. I'm always asking my family to **speak up** – they often sound as if they're **whispering**. **Background noise** is a real problem too – I **don't catch** much of what people are saying in noisy places. Increasingly I have to try and **lip-read**, and I use **subtitles** to watch films on TV.

I know there are certain sounds I'll miss as my hearing gets worse: the **rustling** of autumn leaves; my kids **splashing about** in the pool; my old dog **barking**, and so on. Still, I definitely won't miss the **din** my kids make, **slamming** doors and **yelling at** each other, or the constant **rumble** of traffic. Or my wife's **snoring**!'

WORD FOCUS

If you are **totally deaf**, you cannot hear anything; if you are **partially deaf**, you cannot hear very well. SYN **hard of hearing**. If you are **going deaf**, you are losing your ability to hear. **deafness** N.

be exposed to sth not be protected from
    sth harmful or unpleasant.

hearing your ability to hear.

at full blast as loudly as possible.

lyrics the words of a song.

speak up speak more loudly.

whisper (sth) say sth very quietly so that
    only people close to you can hear it.

background noise noise you can hear but
    are not (directly) listening to.

not catch sth not hear sth that is said,
    often because it is said quickly or quietly.

lip-read understand what sb says by
    watching their lips move.

subtitles words you see at the bottom of
    the screen in a film or on TV. (They
    help deaf people or are used as a
    translation.)

rustling the sound of light, dry things
    moving together. rustle v.

splash about move around noisily in
    water making it go everywhere.

bark when a dog barks, it makes a short,
    loud noise.

din a loud, unpleasant noise which lasts a
    long time.

slam sth if you slam a door, window,
    etc., you shut it with force making a
    loud noise.

yell (at sb) shout loudly at sb.

rumble a long, deep sound: *a rumble of
    thunder*. rumble v.

snoring the noisy breathing sound of sb
    who is asleep. snore v.

Taste

How was your meal at "**Zenos**"? Tell us

Dad had a vegetarian dish: it was full of **spicy flavours**, but not too **hot**.   Jan

It was a **tasty** meal, and obviously made with really fresh **ingredients**.   Su

The beef was a real disappointment – **chewy▼** and rather **tasteless**. In fact, it was almost **inedible**.   Andi

The starter was **so-so**, but then I had the chicken. I **swallowed▼** a **mouthful** and it had the most terrible **aftertaste**. I couldn't eat the rest!   Li

I had French onion soup which was **delicious** and very **authentic**.   Boo

I tried their special bread; the **texture** was OK, but it tasted **artificial** and it was a bit **stale**.   Lorrie

I**'ve got a sweet tooth**, but the dessert was very **sickly**. And the coffee afterwards was a bit **weak**.   Ali

WORD FOCUS

You use your teeth to **bite** (= cut with your teeth) food: *She bit a piece of apple.* **bite** N. You **chew** food to make smaller pieces in your mouth before you **swallow** it (see p.15). If something is **chewy**, you have to chew it for a long time.

spicy having strong flavours from spices,
     e.g. paprika, coriander, ginger.

flavour a particular taste.

hot containing pepper or chilli and
     causing a burning feeling in your
     mouth. OPP mild.

tasty having a strong, pleasant flavour.

ingredients the different food items which
     are put together to make a dish.

tasteless having little or no flavour.

inedible too unpleasant to eat. OPP edible.

so-so INF OK, but not good.

swallow sth make food move from your
     mouth, down your throat, into your
     stomach.

mouthful an amount of food you put in
     your mouth at one time.

aftertaste a taste, often an unpleasant one,
     that stays in your mouth after eating or
     drinking sth.

delicious having a very pleasant taste or
     smell.

authentic if a dish tastes authentic, it tastes
     like an original or traditional example.

texture the way food feels in your mouth
     when you eat it.

artificial not natural.

stale (of bread, cakes, etc.) not fresh.

have (got) a sweet tooth enjoy food that
     has a lot of sugar in it.

sickly unpleasantly sweet.

weak (of coffee, tea, etc.) containing too
     much water and not enough coffee, tea,
     etc. OPP strong.

Sight

One of my roles as a police officer is to carry out **surveillance** on criminal activity. Fortunately, I have perfect **eyesight** and excellent powers of **observation**. As part of the investigation into Lou Green's case, I was sent to **keep watch on** his house. I parked nearby and sat **unobtrusively** in the passenger seat, wearing a **disguise** ▼ so that if Green walked by and **glanced at** me, he wouldn't **recognize** me.

At 22.30, Green drove up to the front door and quickly **disappeared** inside. I was sure he hadn't **noticed** my car or **spotted** anything unusual. I could **just make out** his movements through the curtains. At 22.55, he **stared** out of the window, clearly **on the lookout for** someone. Suddenly, a taxi arrived, and Green moved **out of sight**. I **caught a glimpse of** his visitor entering the house, with what looked like a violin case…

WORD FOCUS

A **disguise** is something you wear or use to change your appearance so that nobody will recognize you; you go out **in disguise**. You can **disguise yourself as sb/sth**: *He disguised himself as a waiter.*

surveillance the act of watching a person suspected of a crime.

eyesight the ability to see.

observation the act of watching sb/sth carefully for a period of time. observe sb/sth v.

keep watch (on sth/sb) watch sth/sb carefully so that you are ready to act if necessary.

unobtrusively in a way that doesn't attract attention.

glance at sb/sth look quickly at sb/sth. glance N: *have a quick glance at sth*.

recognize sb know who sb is when you see or hear them, because you have seen or heard them before.

disappear become impossible to see. SYN vanish. OPP appear.

notice sth see sth and be aware of it.

spot sb/sth see sb/sth suddenly when they are not easy to see.

make sth out see sth with difficulty. (often used with just for emphasis.)

stare (at sth/sb) look at sb/sth very directly for a long time. stare N.

on the lookout for sb/sth watching carefully for sb/sth.

out of sight where sb/sth cannot be seen. OPP in sight.

catch a glimpse of sb/sth see sb/sth for a very short time. SYN glimpse sb/sth.

Touch

press

punch

stroke

squeeze

pinch

tap

nudge

rub

massage

press you press any part of a machine to make it work, e.g. a computer key, or a button in a lift to go up/down.

punch if you punch sth/sb, you hit them hard with your fist (= your tightly closed hand.) punch N.

stroke you stroke sb's hair or an animal's fur (= animal hair) by moving your hand gently and slowly over it, often to show affection. You can also pat an animal (= touch it gently several times with your hand flat, usually to show affection).

squeeze you squeeze sth, e.g. a sponge (see picture), by pressing it firmly.

pinch you can pinch sb hard (= with force so that it hurts) or lightly.

tap you tap sb on the arm or shoulder quickly and lightly to get their attention (= get them to listen to you or look at you).

nudge if you nudge sb, you give them a little push with your elbow (see picture), often to draw their attention to sth/sb (= make them look at sth/sb).

rub when you rub sth, you move your hands over its surface while pressing on it. You can rub cream into your skin with your hands or fingertips (= the ends of your fingers).

massage you massage sb's body by pressing, squeezing or rubbing it in order to reduce pain or relax them. massage N. You can do it gently, firmly or vigorously (= with energy).

2.5 Smell

Pleasant

I love **scented** candles and the **delicate fragrance** of roses.

I've got an **air freshener** in my car which **smells ▼ of citrus fruits**.

That **perfume** has a very **faint smell ▼** of ginger, but I prefer this one – have a **sniff** and tell me what you think!

I love the **aroma** of fresh coffee.

The smell of my wife's perfume **lingers** in the room long after she's gone.

Unpleasant

There's a **funny** smell in the cupboard – it's a bit **musty** in there.

I find certain smells really unpleasant – **sour** milk, for instance, and I can't stand the smell of **stale** cigarette smoke.

When I went in the basement, it **stank** of **rotten** food; it was quite **nauseating**.

WORD FOCUS

Notice the way **smell** N, V is used.
A strong smell of paint.
It smells sweet/nice. [+ ADJ]
This smells of leather. [of + N]
It smells like grass. [like + N]
Can you smell gas in here? [+ N]

scented having a strong, pleasant smell.
  scent N.

delicate light and pleasant. SYN subtle.

fragrance a nice smell (often used about
  flowers or perfume) fragrant ADJ.

air freshener a substance used for making
  a room or car smell nice.

citrus fruit a fruit belonging to the
  group that includes lemons, oranges,
  limes, etc.

perfume a sweet-smelling liquid you put
  on your body to make yourself smell
  pleasant.

faint not easily smelled, seen or heard.
  OPP strong.

sniff a quick breath in through the nose to
  smell sth. sniff sth V.

aroma a strong but pleasant smell (often
  used about food).

linger last longer than expected.

funny strange, and usually unpleasant.
  SYN peculiar.

musty smelling damp and unpleasant
  because of a lack of fresh air.

sour milk or other food that is sour is not
  fresh and has a bad taste and smell.

stale no longer fresh.

stink (of sth) have a strong, unpleasant
  smell. stink N.

rotten (of food) old and not fresh enough
  to eat.

nauseating making you feel sick.
  SYN disgusting.

Physical feelings

If you're worn out,	you're very tired because you've been doing physical exercise or working. SYNS exhausted, shattered INF.
If you're starving INF	you're feeling very hungry.
If you're dying for a drink, INF	you're extremely thirsty. SYN parched INF.
If you're feeling dizzy,	you feel as if everything around you is turning and you can't balance. SYN giddy.
If you're feeling nauseous,	you feel as if you want to vomit (=bring up food from your stomach). SYN (feel) sick.
If you're boiling,	you're feeling very hot. OPP freezing.
If you feel drowsy,	you're feeling relaxed and sleepy, perhaps because it is very warm or you have taken some medicine.
If you're energetic,	you have a lot physical strength and enthusiasm. energy N.

If you're lethargic, you haven't got any energy or enthusiasm.

If you're wide awake, you are completely awake. OPP fast asleep.

If you're shivering, your body is shaking slightly, usually because you are cold or ill.

If you're trembling, your body is shaking slightly, usually because you are frightened.

If you're feeling restless, you can't keep still because you are bored, worried or impatient.

If you're on edge, you're nervous and can't relax because you are worried. SYN tense.

If you've got pins and needles in your leg/foot, etc., you have slight, sharp pains in a part of your body, usually when you move after being in one position for a long time. Also, my foot/leg has gone to sleep.

Reactions

How was the World Cup for you?

'I **could hardly wait** for it to start, but I was **bored**▼ **to death** by most matches. I was so **fed up** that I stopped watching.'

'The opening ceremony **took my breath away**; I was really **impressed**.'

'I was so **relieved** when we won our first game, but **gutted** that we lost to Italy.'

'It was **astonishing**▼ that Brazil didn't do better. I was **stunned** when I heard they'd lost.'

'The **joy** of victory was **overshadowed** by the news of the coach crash.'

'The **noise** at the matches **got on my nerves**, and it **drove** my mum **mad**!'

'All I felt was **frustration**. How could our team be so useless? **No wonder** we lost. I was **furious**.'

'We won! We're all **ecstatic**!' ⚽

WORD FOCUS

Some adjectives have -**ed** or -**ing** endings which describe how we feel or the effect something has on us: bored/boring, astonishing/astonished, etc. Some adjectives only have -**ed**, e.g. relieved (not ~~relieving~~), gutted (not ~~gutting~~). If you are impressed by/with sth, it is impressive (not ~~impressing~~).

can hardly wait used to say that you are very excited about sth you expect to happen.

bored to death extremely bored. SYNS bored stiff/bored rigid/bored to tears.

fed up annoyed or bored by sth that has continued for too long.

take your breath away be very surprising or beautiful. breathtaking ADJ.

impressed admiring sth or sb very much because they are particularly good. impressive ADJ, impress sb V.

relieved happy because sth bad has not happened or a bad situation has ended. relief N.

gutted INF extremely sad and disappointed.

astonishing very surprising. astonish sb V.

stunned shocked and surprised.

joy great happiness. OPP sorrow.

overshadow sth make an event less enjoyable than it should be.

get on your nerves INF if sth gets on your nerves, it annoys you.

drive you mad/crazy INF make you extremely angry or upset.

frustration a feeling of annoyance or impatience when you cannot do or have what you want. frustrated ADJ.

no wonder (that) = it is not surprising (that).

furious very angry. fury N. SYN rage.

ecstatic very happy. SYNS elated/over the moon INF.

Likes and dislikes

Trixie Lux:
her loves and **pet hates**

MUSIC I'm really **into** Cuban music right now. I **loathe** boy bands, girl bands, etc.

ART I **adore** most modern art, but photorealism **leaves me cold**.

FILMS I **detest** films that glorify violence, and I'm **not mad about** thrillers either. I'm **a big fan of** films that deal with political issues in an interesting way.

MEN I **go for** stable, mature men. Guys who treat women badly **disgust me**.

PETS Cats! They're **adorable**. Anything with a cold skin is **vile**, though! I **can't bear** birds in cages – that's just cruel.

FREE TIME I'm **passionate about** outdoor pursuits and keeping fit. Computer games **don't appeal to** me at all – they're just **a waste of time**.

FOOD I get **cravings for** chocolate which is a disaster! I love fish, but I find seafood **revolting**.

TRAVEL I'm **fascinated** by other cultures and I love travelling, but I **have no desire to** live abroad.

pet hate sth that you particularly dislike or that makes you very angry.

be into sth INF be interested in sth.

loathe sth/sb dislike sth/sb very much. SYN detest sth/sb.

adore sth/sb love sth/sb very much. adorable ADJ.

leave sb cold not interest or excite sb.

(not) mad about sth/sb INF (not) liking sth very much.

fan a person who enjoys watching or listening to sb/sth very much: *a big fan of sb/sth.*

go for sb/sth INF like a particular type of person or thing.

disgust sb be so unpleasant as to make sb feel shocked or ill. disgusting ADJ.

vile INF extremely bad or unpleasant.

can't bear sth/sb dislike sth/sb very much. SYNS hate/can't stand sb/sth.

passionate (about sth) having very strong feelings or beliefs about sth.

(not) appeal to sb (not) attract or interest sb.

a waste of time, money, etc. a bad way to use time, money, etc.

craving (for sth) a strong, even uncontrollable, feeling of wanting sth.

revolting extremely unpleasant; making you feel slightly ill. SYN repulsive.

fascinated very interested. fascination N.

desire a strong wish. have no desire to do sth = not want to do sth.

Anger

ANGER is always a **mixture** of feelings: it can **stem from depression**, **guilt**, disappointment, feeling **bitter**, not feeling **valued** or being just plain **weary**. If you are an angry parent or boss, though, it is **crucial** not to **lose your temper** ▼ with your children or colleagues.

You need to recognize your body signals when anger is **building up**, and act before it **gets out of control**. Find the best ways to **cool down** when you're most likely to **lose patience** ▼ : count to ten, or concentrate on breathing slowly. That way, you'll **cope** better **with** stressful situations.

Don't **bottle up** your **emotions**; talk to someone and try to find out the **underlying** causes. If necessary, **seek** the help of a professional **counsellor**. ✛

WORD FOCUS

If you **lose your temper**, you cannot control your anger and may shout at sb. OPP **keep your temper**. You **lose patience** when you have had to wait for a long time, which makes you angry. You might **go mad** INF, or **go berserk** INF = become very angry and not be able to control your anger.

mixture a combination of different things.

stem from sth be the result of sth.

depression a medical condition in which sb is so unhappy they cannot live a normal life. depressed ADJ.

guilt an unhappy feeling caused by knowing or thinking that you have done sth wrong.

bitter feeling angry or unhappy because you have been treated unfairly. bitterness N.

valued useful or important.

weary very tired, especially after working hard. weariness N.

crucial extremely important. SYN vital.

build up become greater or more powerful.

get/be out of control become/be impossible to manage or control.

cool down become calmer. SYN calm down.

cope with sth deal successfully with sth.

bottle sth up hide your feelings (e.g. sadness or anger) over a long period of time.

emotion a strong feeling, e.g. love, anger, or fear. emotional ADJ.

underlying an underlying cause of sth is the real or basic, but it is not easily seen or clearly stated.

seek sth/sb FML look for sth/sb.

counsellor a person whose job is to give advice and help people with problems, especially personal problems.

Tears and laughter

'My brother used to **make fun of me** because of my curly hair. It seemed to **amuse** him, but it really **upset** me. One day he started **teasing** me in front of my friends and I just **burst into tears**. He knew he'd **gone too far** and said sorry.'

'We watched the film 'Titanic' the other night and my sister **cried her eyes out**. She was still **sobbing** an hour later!'

'When I was a kid, dad used to **tickle** me, which made me **giggle** a lot.'

'My colleague Tom is always **telling jokes** ▼; he has everyone **in stitches**!'

'Dave read the letter, then looked up, **grinning from ear to ear**. We knew immediately he'd got the job.'

'Jo told me I'd won, but she was just **pulling my leg**. She can be very **mean**.'

'I **laughed my head off** when Bill fell over, but he didn't think it was funny, and the others all **frowned at** me.'

WORD FOCUS

If you **tell a joke**, you say something funny to make people laugh, e.g. a funny story. If you don't understand a joke, you don't **get** it. If a joke **falls flat**, nobody laughs.

make fun of sb make jokes about sb, often in an unkind way. SYN poke fun at sb.

amuse sb make sb laugh or smile.

upset sb make sb feel unhappy or worried. upset ADJ.

tease sb say sth to sb in the form of a playful joke.

burst into tears suddenly begin to cry. (Also burst out laughing = suddenly begin to laugh.)

go too far behave in an extreme way that is not acceptable.

cry your eyes out cry a lot, or for a long time.

sob cry noisily taking sudden, deep breaths. sob N.

tickle sb touch sb lightly and repeatedly so that they laugh.

giggle laugh in an excited or silly way, with high-pitched, rapid sounds, because you are amused, embarrassed or nervous.

in stitches INF laughing a lot. have sb/be in stitches.

grin smile widely: grin from ear to ear smile very widely. grin N.

pull sb's leg INF tell sb sth that is not true, as a joke. SYN have sb on INF.

mean (of a person or their behaviour) unkind.

laugh your head off laugh loudly for a long time. SYN roar with laughter.

frown (at sb) make a serious, worried or angry face by pulling your eyebrows together.

Personal statements

I believe I am a very **straightforward, level-headed** sort of person who can be **relied on** in any circumstances.

I am **positive** in every aspect of my life, and **adventurous by nature,** ready to **take up** any challenge I am given.

I am very **aware of** my **strengths** and **weaknesses**. People say I am **dynamic** and **creative**, but I have a **reputation** for being **over-enthusiastic**.

I would describe myself as a highly **motivated** teacher who **takes** her responsibilities very **seriously**. I try hard to be **sensitive** ▼ to my students' needs.

I am **dedicated** and **live for** my work; I guarantee complete **loyalty** to the firm.

See page 252 for information on writing personal statements.

WORD FOCUS

A **sensitive** person understands people's feelings and is kind to them: *I try to be sensitive with colleagues.* **Sensitive** also means 'easily hurt or upset': *She's sensitive, so don't shout at her.*
Don't confuse this with a **sensible** person who makes good decisions about things: *He's very sensible; he's brought an umbrella in case it rains.*

straightforward honest and open.

level-headed calm and able to deal easily with difficult situations.

rely on sb trust sb to do sth for you.

positive believing good things will happen. OPP negative.

adventurous not afraid of taking risks or trying new things.

by nature in character.

take sth up accept sth that is offered.

aware of sth knowing or realizing sth.

strength a particular quality or ability. OPP weakness.

dynamic having a lot of energy and a strong personality.

creative having new or imaginative ideas.

reputation the opinion that people have about sb/sth based on what has happened in the past: *a good/bad reputation*.

over-enthusiastic showing too much excitement and interest in sth.

motivated a motivated person is very interested and works hard.

take sth seriously think that sth is important and should have your attention.

dedicated working hard at sth because it is very important to you. SYN committed. dedication N.

live for sth think that sth is the most important thing in your life.

loyalty constant support you give sb/sth because you feel duty or love towards them.

School report

TOM BAXTER • Year 8

Science: Tom shows great **curiosity** about science, but is very **disorganized** in his work.

Maths: Tom is a **capable** boy, but is easily **distracted** by other students in the class.

English: Tom is **eager** ▼ and **determined** to do well. He has a **flair** for language, but his **careless** spelling **lets him down**.

History: Tom is **gaining in confidence** and is making good progress.

Sport: He is highly **competitive** in all sports and shows great **potential** as a footballer.

Art: Tom **makes** little **effort** and spends too much time in class **showing off** in front of other boys. He needs to be more **mature** and **responsible**.

Overall: A **likeable** student, Tom is **conscientious** in some areas but not others; he needs to be more **consistent**.

WORD FOCUS

If you are **eager** to do something, you are excited by it and really want to do it. SYN **keen. eagerness** N. The opposite is **reluctant**: *He was reluctant to dive into the water.*

curiosity a strong desire to know about sth.
disorganized not able to plan things in a
    clear and sensible way. OPP organized.
capable having the ability to do things well.
distracted unable to pay attention because
    you are thinking about sth else.
determined having such a strong desire
    to do sth that you will not let anybody
    stop you.
flair a natural ability to do sth well.
careless lacking thought or planning so
    that you make mistakes. carelessness N.
let sb down If sth lets you down, it makes
    you less successful than you should be.
gain in sth get more of a particular quality.
confidence a belief in your ability to do
    sth and be successful. confident ADJ.
competitive wanting very much to win or
    be more successful than other people.
potential your ability to develop or succeed.
make no/little effort not try hard enough
    to do sth that is difficult.
show off INF try to impress other people
    by talking about your abilities in a way
    that can be annoying.
mature behaving in a sensible way, like an
    adult. OPP immature.
responsible sensible, reliable and able to
    be trusted. OPP irresponsible.
likeable pleasant and easy to like.
conscientious taking care to do things
    carefully and correctly.
consistent always behaving in the same
    way or having the same standards.

4.3

Behaviour

I was a **studious, well-behaved** ▼ child, which was lucky because my parents were **strict**. I was quite **shy** and **blushed** easily (I still do). My teachers said I was very **bright** and I always had my head in a book. But I was **hopeless at** games and very **clumsy**, always dropping things.

Despite having the same **upbringing**, my sister was completely different. She was a real **tomboy**: she **couldn't be bothered to** work hard and just wanted to play outside. At school the teachers said she was very **naughty**, ▼ and she **was** always **in trouble** for being **cheeky**.

Our older brother **looked down on** my sister and me and thought we were **irritating**. At the time, he was **bossy** and **impatient** with us, but these days, we all get on really well.

WORD FOCUS

Children are often described as being **well behaved** (= acting in a way that is polite and gentle and does not upset people) or **badly behaved**. A child who **misbehaves** (= behaves badly) may be described as **naughty** or **disobedient** (= refusing to obey rules) OPP **obedient**. **obey sb** V.

studious spending a lot of time studying or reading.

strict demanding that rules of behaviour should be obeyed. OPP lenient.

shy nervous and embarrassed when meeting and speaking to people, especially people you do not know.

blush become red in the face because you are embarrassed.

bright intelligent and quick to learn.

hopeless at sth INF very bad at sth.

clumsy moving in a way that is not careful or graceful, and sometimes breaking things.

upbringing the care and instruction of children by their parents as they grow up.

tomboy a girl who does activities that people think are more suitable for boys.

can't be bothered INF if you can't be bothered to do sth, you are too lazy or tired to do it.

be in/get into trouble be in or get into a situation for which you are likely to be blamed, criticized or punished.

cheeky rude in a funny or disrespectful way.

look down on sb think you are better or more important than sb else.

irritating making you feel annoyed or impatient.

bossy always telling people what to do in a way that annoys them.

impatient irritated by sb/sth, especially because you have had to wait a long time.

TV characters

In **soap operas**, certain types of **character** ▼ are common:

- The **tough** woman: an **aggressive** woman, always at the centre of conflict. Often has **a** hidden **soft side** to her **character**▼, especially when she is unlucky in love.

- The grandparent: a **supportive figure**▼ who is **respected** by everyone for their **wisdom**.

- The **villain**: usually an **arrogant** young man; a **liar** who **manipulates** people.

- The **strong-willed** young woman: a character who **longs for independence**. Often **argumentative**.

- The **bad-tempered** older person: someone who is always **interfering** and **poking their nose into** other people's business, but often has a good heart.

WORD FOCUS

Character has different meanings.
1 a person in a book, film, play, etc.:
The doctor is an important character in the film.
2 the set of qualities that make a person who they are: *Honesty is an essential part of his character.*

A **figure** is someone who is important in some way: *a key political figure.*

soap opera a series of TV stories about the lives of an imaginary group of people.

tough strong enough to deal with difficult situations.

aggressive angry and showing you want to fight or argue with sb.

a soft side a gentle part of your character.

supportive helping or encouraging sb.

respected if you are respected, other people have a good opinion of you.

wisdom the ability to make good decisions based on your experience and knowledge.

villain the main bad character in a story.

arrogant thinking you are better than others and behaving in a way that is too confident.

liar a person who does not tell the truth.

manipulate sb control or influence sb, often in a dishonest way.

strong-willed very determined to do what you want to do.

long for sth want sth very much.

independence the freedom to organize your life and make decisions without help from others. **independent** ADJ.

argumentative an argumentative person likes disagreeing with others.

bad-tempered often in an angry mood.

interfere (in sth) get involved in a situation and try to influence the way it develops, although you have no right to do this.

poke your nose into sth If you poke your nose into sth, you are interfering in sth.

Opposites

What are you like?

Look at the opposites and tick ✓ the box which best represents you!

very . . .	◄· · · · · · · ·►	very . . .
generous	☐ ✓ ☐ ☐	mean
competent	☐ ☐ ☐ ☐	incompetent
courageous	☐ ☐ ☐ ☐	cowardly
cautious	☐ ☐ ☐ ☐	reckless
considerate	☐ ☐ ☐ ☐	thoughtless
decisive	☐ ☐ ☐ ☐	indecisive
outgoing	☐ ☐ ☐ ☐	shy
easy-going	☐ ☐ ☐ ☐	uptight
cheerful	☐ ☐ ☐ ☐	gloomy
approachable	☐ ☐ ☐ ☐	unapproachable
selfish	☐ ☐ ☐ ☐	selfless
modest	☐ ☐ ☐ ☐	conceited
secure	☐ ☐ ☐ ☐	lacking in confidence ▼

WORD FOCUS

If you **lack sth, are lacking in sth**, or have **a lack of sth**, you do not have it, or do not have as much of it as you need.
She's qualified, but lacks experience.
He's lacking in common sense.
His problem was a lack of effort.

generous willing to give or share things, especially money. OPPS mean, stingy INF.

competent having the ability or skills to do sth well. SYN able. OPP incompetent.

courageous showing no fear of dangerous or difficult things. SYN brave. OPP cowardly.

cautious careful about what you say or do and not willing to take risks. OPPS reckless, rash.

considerate caring about the feelings and needs of others. OPPS thoughtless, inconsiderate.

decisive able to make choices or decide what to do quickly and confidently. OPP indecisive.

outgoing friendly and liking to meet and talk to other people. SYN extrovert. OPPS shy, diffident.

easy-going relaxed and not easily upset or worried. SYN laid back. INF. OPP uptight INF.

cheerful happy and showing it in the way you behave. OPP gloomy.

approachable friendly and easy to talk to. OPP unapproachable.

selfish caring only about yourself and not other people. OPP selfless.

modest APPROVING not talking much about your own abilities or success. OPP conceited DISAPPROVING.

secure feeling confident and with no anxiety. OPPS lacking in confidence, insecure.

Neighbours

What are your **neighbours** ▼ like?

'Brilliant. We **socialize with** a lot of our neighbours, and there's a real **community spirit**. One of them **keeps an eye on** our house while we're away.'

'I live **on my own**, but I know I can **count on** my **next-door neighbour** ▼. He's always ready to **lend a hand** when I need help. You hear a lot about the **breakdown** of communities, but that's not my experience.'

'I don't **mix with** people in my **neighbourhood** ▼. I like my **privacy**, and I hate all the **gossiping** that goes on.'

'Where I used to live, there was a lot of **vandalism** and **antisocial behaviour** by **gangs** of **youths**. I've moved to a new **council estate**, where people are very **neighbourly** ▼ and behave in a much more **civil** manner towards each other.'

WORD FOCUS

Your **neighbours** are people who live near you; your **next-door neighbour** is your closest neighbour. A **neighbourhood** is an area in a town where people live. A **neighbourly** area is one where people are kind and help each other.

socialize (with sb) spend a lot of time with people in a friendly way. SYN mix with sb. sociable ADJ.

community all the people who live in a particular area.

spirit loyal feelings towards a group, team, community, etc.

keep an eye on sth watch sth to make sure that it is not harmed or damaged.

on your own alone. SYN by yourself.

count on sb trust sb to do sth.

lend (sb) a hand INF help sb.

breakdown a situation in which sth is failing.

privacy a state in which other people cannot see you or know what you are doing. private ADJ.

gossiping the act of talking about other people in a way that may be unkind or not true. gossip N,V.

vandalism the crime of destroying or damaging sth for no reason. The person who does this is a vandal.

antisocial behaviour a way of behaving that harms or annoys other people.

gang a group of young people who often cause trouble or fight against each other.

youth OFTEN DISAPPROVING a young man.

council estate a large group of houses built by the local council (= the people who are elected to govern an area such as a town).

civil polite, often in a formal way, but possibly not friendly.

Friendship

Dear **agony aunt**

When I moved to a new area last year, I **got in with** a **circle** of friends through my job. We're not **close**, but we **keep** each other **company**, listen to each other's **concerns**, **have a laugh**, etc.

I recently discovered that they've **met up** without **inviting** me **along**. I know I'm a bit of a **loner**, but I felt **hurt** that no one had thought to ask me, and to be honest, I'm a bit **envious** of the way they get on. I must admit I'm quite lazy with **friendships**: I don't **take the initiative** and invite people out, but on the other hand, I **treat** people **with respect**. I will see them again soon, but should I **bring up** the fact that they didn't invite me?

Conrad

Hi Conrad,

I don't recommend **drawing attention to** the situation. Has it **occurred to** you that perhaps they feel hurt too that you don't seem to **take the first step**? All relationships have their **ups and downs**, but if you want your **acquaintances** to become friends, you should perhaps make more effort yourself.

Good luck!

agony aunt (in a newspaper, etc.) sb who gives advice to people with personal problems.

get in with sb INF become friendly with sb.

circle a group of people who are connected.

close knowing sb well and liking them.

keep sb company spend time with sb so that they are not alone.

concern sth that worries you.

have a laugh INF have an enjoyable time.

meet up (with sb) meet sb, usually by arrangement.

invite sb along ask sb to go somewhere with you and other people.

loner a person who prefers to be alone.

hurt made to feel upset or unhappy.

envious wanting to be in the same situation as sb else, or wanting sth that sb else has.

friendship a relationship between friends.

take the initiative take action before other people do so. SYN take the first step.

treat sb with respect behave towards sb in a polite way that shows that you admire their good qualities or achievements.

bring sth up start to talk about a subject.

draw attention to sth make sb notice sth.

occur to sb if an idea occurs to you, you suddenly start to think about it.

ups and downs a mixture of good and bad things in life or in a relationship.

acquaintance a person you know, but who is not a close friend.

How we met

LUCY I met Carlo on **a blind date**, actually. We started talking and **hit it off** straightaway – we **had** so much **in common**. At that stage, I wasn't looking for **romance**, nor **was** I really **attracted to** him, but he was **good company.** There was no **flirting**, and I didn't feel he was trying to **chat me up**, which was a **refreshing** change**.**

CARLO I could see that Lucy hadn't exactly **fallen for** me, but that didn't matter. I don't really believe in **love at first sight** anyway. Lucy had a dog, so we started going for walks together, and **little by little**, we **grew to like** each other more and more. And now I'm just **crazy about** her! I think we're both glad that we didn't **rush into** anything. But last week I **proposed,** and I'm delighted to say she's now my **fiancée!**

a blind date a meeting between two people who have never met before. They spend time together to see if a romance develops.

hit it off (with sb) INF immediately have a good, friendly relationship with sb.

have sth in common (with sb) (of two people) have interests that are the same.

romance an exciting relationship between two people who are in love. romantic ADJ.

be attracted to sb be interested in sb in a romantic way.

good company a person who is good company is pleasant to be with.

flirting the action of behaving towards sb as if you find them attractive. flirt v.

chat sb up INF talk in a friendly way to sb that you are attracted to.

refreshing pleasantly new and different.

fall for sb INF be strongly attracted to sb.

love at first sight love you feel the first time you see sb.

little by little slowly; gradually.

grow to like sb/sth slowly begin to like sb/sth.

crazy/mad about sb INF liking sb very much; being in love with sb.

rush into sth do sth without thinking about it carefully.

propose (to sb) ask sb to marry you.

fiancée the woman that a man is engaged to and will marry; the man is her fiancé. (These words come from French.)

5.4

Wedding guests

Seating at the reception

- At the **reception,** the **bride** and **groom,** their parents, the **best man,** and the **bridesmaids** very often sit together at the top table.

- The bride and groom's **immediate families** are usually **seated** at two tables near the top table. These include **siblings,** grandparents, and other close **relations.** Be careful about family politics, especially with **divorced** parents, **stepmother** ▼ **or father** or **in-laws** who do not get on. Putting **extended family** members together is usually a sensible idea.

- Next, consider your friends. If they are **singles,** seat them together or with someone they know so that they don't feel **left out**. Keep **ex-boyfriends** and **ex-girlfriends** apart, unless you know they get on well.

- Find an accessible place for anyone who is **infirm** or who has a **disability.** ■

WORD FOCUS

Your **stepfather** is the man who is married to your mother, but is not your birth father; your **stepbrother** is your **stepfather** or **stepmother**'s son. Also, **stepsister, stepson,** etc.

reception a formal social occasion to welcome sb or celebrate sth: *a wedding reception*.

bride a woman on her wedding day.

groom a man on his wedding day.

best man a close friend or family member who helps the groom at the wedding.

bridesmaid a girl or young woman who helps the bride at the wedding.

immediate family very close family: parents, children, brothers, sisters.

seat sb give sb a place to sit.

sibling a brother or sister.

relation a member of your wider family. SYN relative.

divorced no longer legally married. divorce N, V.

in-laws INF your relatives by marriage, e.g. your wife's brother is your brother-in-law.

extended family not only brothers, sisters, etc., but also nieces, aunts, etc.

singles PL N people who are not married or in a romantic relationship with sb. (Couples are married or in a romantic relationship.)

left out not included in sth.

ex-boyfriend a boyfriend you had in the past who is not your boyfriend now; also ex-girlfriend, ex-wife, etc.

infirm (especially of old people) ill or weak.

disability a condition in which sb cannot use part of their body or brain properly. disabled ADJ.

Marriage

In every **marriage** more than a week old, there are **grounds** for divorce. The **trick** is to find, and continue to find, grounds for marriage.

Robert Anderson

A wedding **anniversary** ▼ is the **celebration** of love, **trust**, **partnership**, **tolerance** and **tenacity**. The order **varies** in any **given** year.

Paul Sweeney

A wedding is just like a **funeral** except that you get to smell your own flowers.

Grace Hansen

Don't marry the person you can live with; marry only the **individual** you think you **can't live without**.

James C. Dodson

It isn't **tying** himself **to** one woman that a man **dreads** when he thinks of marrying; it's **separating** himself **from** all the others.

Helen Rowland

Sometimes I **wonder** if men and women really **suit** each other. Perhaps they should live next door and just visit now and then.

Katherine Hepburn

WORD FOCUS

An **anniversary** is the day that is an exact number of years since a special event happened. We use **birthday**, not **anniversary**, for the day we were born.

50

marriage the relationship between a husband and wife.

grounds PL N a good reason for sth.

trick a good and clever way of doing sth.

celebration an occasion when you do sth enjoyable because of a special event.

trust the belief that sb is good, honest, etc. and will not harm or lie to you.

partnership a relationship between two people, two organizations, etc.

tolerance the willingness to accept sb's opinions, way of life, etc., even if you do not agree with them. **tolerant** ADJ.

tenacity FML a determination to do sth and not give up. **tenacious** ADJ.

vary be different in different situations.

a given (year) a particular (year).

funeral a ceremony that takes place when sb has died.

individual a particular person.

can't live without sb/sth be unable to live happily without a person or thing.

tie sb to sb/sth if you are tied to sb/sth, you cannot leave them and you are unable to do everything you want to do.

dread (doing) sth feel afraid of or unhappy about (doing) sth.

separate sb from sb/sth move sb away or apart from sb/sth.

wonder think about whether sth is true or will happen.

suit sb be right or good for sb/sth.

5.6 Being a parent

Looking after **toddlers**:
As a parent, you spend a lot of time **establishing** a **routine** of sleep, eating, play, etc. Expect your child to be **defiant**: it's part of becoming more independent. And be prepared for **sibling rivalry!**

Primary school children:
At this age, they begin to **copy behaviour** that they **admire**. This is the time to work on **confidence building**, as well as **encouraging** them to live **in harmony with** their brothers and sisters. You also need to look for any signs of **bullying**.

Teens▼:
This can be a very **challenging** time for you and your children. Most **teenagers** ▼ are wonderful, but they can suffer from **mood swings** as they move from **adolescence** ▼ to **adulthood. Anxiety** about their appearance is common, as is **peer pressure**: your teenagers will need guidance, but also **space** to make mistakes.

WORD FOCUS

Teenagers, also **teens** INF, are people aged between 13 and 19. An **adolescent** is a teenager; this word focuses on the development from childhood to adulthood. **Adolescence** refers to that period of time.

toddler a child who has just learnt to walk.

establish sth start or create sth, e.g. a system, that is meant to last for a long time.

routine the normal order or way in which you regularly do sth.

defiant refusing to obey sb or a rule.

sibling rivalry competition between sisters and brothers, e.g. for their parents' love.

copy sth do sth in the same way as sb else.

behaviour acting or doing things in a particular way. behave v.

admire sth/sb feel great respect for sth/sb.

confidence building helping sb to believe that they can be successful.

encourage sb to do sth give sb support or hope that they can do sth.

in harmony with sb in a situation in which people live and work well with other people.

bullying behaviour that frightens or hurts sb smaller or weaker. The person who does this is a bully. bully sb v.

challenging difficult to deal with.

mood swing a change of mood, e.g. from happy or friendly to sad or angry.

adulthood the state of being an adult.

anxiety the state of feeling nervous or worried that sth bad is going to happen. anxious ADJ.

peer pressure the influence that other people of the same age have on you.

space freedom and time to do what you want.

5.7 Family history

I'm American, and I've been trying to **trace** my **roots** back to my Italian **ancestors**. My **great grandfather** was the **only child** of Italian **immigrants** ▼ who came to the US in the early 1900s and **settled** in New York. This was a time when there was **large-scale emigration** ▼ from Italy because of disease and **poverty**.

I've recently **inherited** an old wooden box which has been **passed down** through several **generations** of my family. It contains **birth** and **death certificates**, a **family tree**, as well as old family photos. I've noticed some clear family **resemblances**: my brothers obviously **take after** Great Grandpa with their thick, curly hair. In fact, all his **descendants** have the same handsome nose! Next year I plan to travel to Italy to look at various historical **records**. ∎

WORD FOCUS

An **immigrant** is someone who has come from their country to live permanently in another country. The process is called **immigration**; the opposite is **emigration** (= going to live in a different country from your own). **emigrate** v.

trace sth (back to sth) find the origin of
    sth (=where sth begins or comes from).

roots the place and people you come from.

ancestor sb in your family who lived a
    long time ago.

great grandfather the father of your
    grandparent; great grandmother/
    aunt, etc.

only child sb with no brothers or sisters.

settle (somewhere) go to live
    permanently in a place.

scale the size of sth, especially when it is
    big or small: *large-/small-scale*.

poverty the state of being very poor.

inherit sth receive money, property, etc.
    from sb when they die. inheritance N.

pass sth down give an object, knowledge,
    etc. to your children or to younger people.

generation all the people who were born
    at about the same time.

birth certificate a formal document that
    states when and where you were born.
    Also death certificate.

family tree a diagram that shows the
    relationship between family members
    over different generations.

resemblance similarity of appearance.
    resemble sb/sth v.

take after sb look or behave like an older
    member of your family.

descendant your descendants are your
    children, and your children's children, etc.

record a written account of sth that is kept
    and can be read in the future.

Injuries

I've injured my knee by running too much.	hurt a part of your body, often in an accident. injury N.
He had a knife wound, and was bleeding badly.	an injury, especially a cut or hole. wound sb/sth v. If you cut yourself, you bleed (= lose blood from the wound).
She cut her hand and will need stitches.	a short piece of thread that a doctor, nurse, etc. uses to join sb's skin together when it has been cut.
I fell over and grazed my knees on the path.	break the surface of your skin, for example when you fall to the ground. (It does not usually bleed much.)
I sprained my wrist playing tennis.	injure a joint (= a place where two bones meet) with a sudden movement.
She twisted her ankle.	injure part of your body, especially your ankle, wrist or knee, by bending it in the wrong direction.

I pulled a muscle lifting the suitcase.	**injure a muscle** (= a piece of the body tissue that you expand and relax in order to move part of your body).
She had her arm in a sling.	**a band of cloth** you tie round your neck to support an injured arm or wrist.
Jo had a fracture in her leg.	**a broken bone**: a fractured arm/skull (= head bone).
She suffered from severe burns.	**a serious injury** on your body caused by heat or fire. OPP minor burn.
How did you get that bruise on your arm?	**a blue or brown mark** that appears on the skin after you have been hit. bruise sth v. A bruise on your eye is a black eye.
The cat scratched his face badly.	**cut or damage your skin** with something sharp.
These shoes gave me blisters on my heels.	**a small painful area** of skin that looks like a bubble full of liquid.

First aid

To clean a **wound**, you will need **cotton wool** and **antiseptic lotion**. **Bathe** the wound thoroughly. Cover it with a **plaster** or use a clean **dressing** to **prevent infection**▼. Hold the dressing **in place** with a **bandage**.

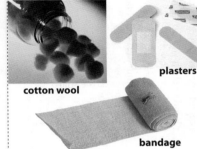

plasters

cotton wool

bandage

If a part of the body is **swollen**, put some frozen peas wrapped in a towel on it to reduce the **swelling**.

For bee **stings**, remove the **sting** with **tweezers**, then put some **antihistamine cream** on it.

tweezers

To **treat** a burn **effectively**, first place it under cool **running water** for 15 minutes.

wound an injury, especially a cut or
    a hole.
antiseptic lotion a special liquid used for
    cleaning wounds.
bathe sth wash a part of your body.
dressing a piece of material put over a
    wound to protect it.
prevent sth (from doing sth) stop sth
    from happening.
in place in the correct position.
swollen larger or rounder than usual
    because of an injury or illness.
    swelling N.
sting 1 the pain you feel when a sharp part
    of an insect, animal or plant enters or
    scratches your skin. 2 the sharp part of
    the bee that stays under your skin.
antihistamine cream a cream used to
    prevent a bad reaction to stings.
treat sth/sb give medical care to sth/sb.
    treatment N.
effectively working well and giving the
    result that was intended.
running water a continuous flow of water
    from a tap.

WORD FOCUS

An **infection** is an illness in part of your
body caused by bacteria or a virus:
an ear/a chest infection. You clean
wounds so that they don't become
infected. If sb is **infectious**, they have a
disease that can be easily passed on to
another person.

6.3 A common illness

Symptoms of HAY FEVER:

- Frequent **sneezing**

sneeze

- A **runny nose**
- **Itchy** eyes
- Generally feeling **unwell**

Diagnosis:

- The symptoms are usually obvious, but in some cases a **blood test** is required.

Over-the-counter remedies:

- **Tablets** to **relieve** a runny nose

tablets SYN pills

- **Nasal sprays** to reduce **inflammation**

nasal spray   injection

Note: **Steroid injections** are not suitable **owing to** unwanted **side effects**.

symptom a sign that sb has an illness.

hay fever an illness caused by a bad reaction to grass or plants (= an allergy) that some people get in the summer.

runny nose a runny nose produces a lot of liquid.

itchy having an uncomfortable feeling on your skin that makes you want to scratch it (= rub it with your nails). itch N, V.

unwell feeling ill/not well.

diagnosis the act of discovering what illness sb has by examining them closely.

blood test an examination of your blood to find out if it shows any sign of illness.

over-the counter medicine/remedies medicine you can buy at the chemist's without a prescription (= an official note from your doctor to a pharmacist saying which medicine you need).

remedy a cure for pain or illness.

relieve sth make a pain or bad feeling get better or stop.

inflammation an area of your body that becomes red, sore and swollen because of infection.

steroid a chemical substance used to treat some diseases.

owing to sth because of sth.

side effect an unpleasant effect that a drug has on your body in addition to curing pain and illness.

Symptoms

I **had a really bad night**, and now I've got an **upset stomach**, a **rash** on my **chest**, and a **temperature** ▼. It's just some 24-hour **bug**, I expect. Or maybe it was something I ate yesterday.

Jessica's got this strange **sensation** in her leg, and her toes feel **numb**. It's a bit worrying, actually. I think it could be some **nerve** damage.

Danny woke up this morning with a **stiff neck** and he was **aching all over**. I think he **overdid** it yesterday playing football.

Mac's been feeling a bit **down** recently. He's **lost his appetite** and he's been **suffering from insomnia**. His doctor thinks he's **depressed**.

Carol's had a very **sore throat** for the last few days, and now she's **lost her voice** completely.

WORD FOCUS

If you**'ve got a temperature**, your body is hotter than normal because you are ill. If your body is <u>much</u> hotter than normal, you have **a high temperature/a fever**.

have a good/bad night sleep well/badly.

an upset stomach an illness which makes you sick or have diarrhoea (= an illness in which you pass waste from your body too often and in a liquid form).

rash an area of small red spots on the skin.

chest the front part of your body, between your neck and stomach.

bug INF a mild, infectious illness. SYN virus.

sensation an unusual feeling in a part of your body.

numb if a part of your body is numb, you cannot feel it. numbness N.

nerve one of the fibres carrying messages between your brain and parts of your body, enabling you to move, feel pain, etc.

stiff if a part of your body is stiff, your muscles hurt when you move: *a stiff neck.*

ache feel a continuous pain which is unpleasant but not very strong. (Also ache all over = ache everywhere.)

overdo sth do sth too much.

down unhappy or depressed. SYN low.

lose your appetite not want to eat for a period of time.

suffer from sth be badly affected by pain, disease, sadness, etc.

insomnia an inability to sleep.

depressed sad and without hope.

sore throat a pain in the part of your neck through which food passes.

lose your voice be unable to speak clearly.

Fainting

A: What happened to Lucia?

B: Well, we were at work and she **bumped** her head **on** a glass door. She seemed OK, but she looked a bit **pale** and started complaining of feeling **dizzy** and **disorientated.** I could see that she was **sweating** and **breathing** very fast, then **all of a sudden**, she just **passed out** ▼ on the floor.

A: Oh, no!

B: When she **came to**, she started **shaking** and said she was **feeling sick;** she ran to the bathroom and **threw up**.

A: Oh dear. Poor Lucia. How long was she **unconscious** ▼?

B: Oh, not long, but after she'd **been sick,** she felt completely **wiped out**.

A: I'm not surprised. I guess the **fainting** ▼ must have been a **reaction** to hitting her head – it can't have **done her any good**.

B: No. Anyway, she's gone to hospital just to get everything **checked out**.

WORD FOCUS

If you **pass out,** you are in a state like sleep because you are ill or injured. SYNS **faint, black out**. When you pass out, you are **unconscious**/you **lose consciousness** (= you cannot hear, feel or think). OPP **conscious**.

64

bump sth (on/against sth) hit sth, especially a part of your body (on/against sth). bump N.

pale if you look pale, your face has little colour because of illness, worry, etc.

dizzy feeling as if everything is turning around and you might fall over. SYN giddy.

disorientated (also disoriented) confused about where you are and unable to think clearly.

sweat produce liquid on the surface of your skin when you are hot, nervous, etc. sweat N.

breathe (in/out) take air into your lungs and send it out again through your nose or mouth.

all of a sudden suddenly.

come to become conscious again. SYNS come round/regain consciousness.

shake move from side to side or up and down with short, quick movements because you are ill, nervous, etc. SYN tremble.

feel sick feel ill in your stomach so that you want to vomit (=bring food from your stomach back out through the mouth). SYN feel nauseous.

throw up vomit. SYN be sick.

wiped out INF extremely tired.

reaction a response by the body, usually a bad one, to sth that has happened.

do sb good be helpful or useful to sb.

check sth out look at or examine sth.

Hospital treatment

'I went to the doctor's **surgery** with a terrible pain in my foot. The doctor **examined** me and **prescribed painkillers**. But after a while, it was obvious that the treatment hadn't worked, so he sent me to hospital for an **x-ray**. Eventually, I saw a **consultant** who **operated on** my foot. I spent six weeks **recuperating** at home.'

an x-ray

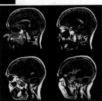

a scan

'My brother was having severe stomach pains and went to **A and E**, where they did a **scan**; he was **diagnosed** with **appendicitis**. He **was admitted** immediately and had an **operation**, but unfortunately there were **complications**. He had to spend a few days on an **intensive care ward**, and it took him weeks to **get over it**.'

surgery the place where a doctor, dentist or vet sees their patients.

examine sb look at sb carefully to see if they are healthy. examination N.

prescribe sth (of a doctor) say what medicine sb should have. prescription N.

painkiller a drug that reduces pain.

consultant a hospital doctor who is an expert in an area of medicine.

operate on sb cut sb's body to treat a part that is damaged or infected. operation N.

recuperate (from sth) get well again after an illness or injury. recuperation N. SYN convalesce V, convalescence N.

A and E ABBREV Accident and Emergency a hospital department where you are taken if you have an accident.

diagnose sth say what an illness or cause of a problem is; (make a) diagnosis N.

appendicitis an illness in which a small organ near your stomach (the appendix) becomes very painful and is removed.

admit sb (to hospital) accept sb in a hospital for medical treatment. (When sb leaves hospital, they are discharged.)

complications a new problem which makes an existing medical condition worse.

intensive care ward a hospital area with beds (=ward) where very sick people go for special care.

get over sth start to feel well again after sth bad has happened. SYN recover (from sth). recovery N.

HEALTH

6.7 Ethical dilemmas

- Thanks to **organ transplants**, many people are given a **new lease of life** through the **altruism** of organ **donors** and their families. But there are two major **ethical** decisions: how should we get the organs, and how should we decide who receives them?

- If someone has been **in a coma** for years and is **on life support,** should their life be **prolonged indefinitely**?

- Some people with an **incurable** or **terminal illness** may have little **quality of life.** They may say that they do not wish to be **resuscitated**. Should doctors ever **override** their wishes?

- **Research ▼** using animals has made a huge contribution to medical advances, but it is still **highly controversial**. Is it ever acceptable to use animals for this purpose?

WORD FOCUS

Research is the detailed study of something in order to discover new facts. It is uncountable, e.g. *He did some research/a piece of research*. NOT <del>researches</del>.
You can *carry out, conduct, do,* or *undertake research*.

ethical relating to beliefs and principles about what is right or wrong.

dilemma a situation in which you have to make a difficult decision.

organ transplant an operation in which an organ, e.g. a heart from sb who has just died, is put into another person's body.

a new lease of life better health or new energy and enthusiasm.

altruism a way of thinking that shows you care for other people, and put their needs before your own. **altruistic** ADJ.

donor sb who gives blood or a part of their body for medical purposes.

in a coma in a state in which sb is unconscious for a long time.

on life support (of a very sick person) being kept alive by special equipment.

prolong sth make sth last longer.

indefinitely for a period of time that has no fixed end.

incurable if sb has an incurable illness, they cannot be made healthy again.

terminal illness an illness that is incurable and eventually causes death.

quality of life the level of enjoyment, health and comfort in your life.

resuscitate sb make sb start breathing again after they have almost died.

override sth use your authority to reject sb else's decision, wishes, etc.

(highly) controversial causing a lot of public discussion. **controversy** N.

Healthy living

HEALTHY EATING: It's not a good idea to be either **overweight** or **underweight**. **Base** your food intake **on starchy foods** such as rice, **wholemeal bread** and pasta. These **contain carbohydrates** ▼: a necessary **source** of energy, and they make you feel **full**. People often think these are **fattening**, but they contain less than half the **calories** of fat. Try to eat at least five **portions** of fruit and vegetables a day, and plenty of fish: a rich source of **proteins** ▼. Avoid **dairy products**: too much cream and cheese can lead to **obesity**.

HEALTHY ACTIVITY: Even if you are **unfit**, it's never too late to take exercise. Everyday activities such as cycling, **brisk** walking, housework, **DIY**, etc. all help. Aim for activities that **boost** strength and help your **coordination** and balance. Try to **ensure** a **minimum** of thirty minutes of **intense** activity several times a week.

WORD FOCUS

Carbohydrates are a substance in food that gives you energy, e.g. rice, potatoes. **Protein** is a substance in food such as fish or eggs that keeps you healthy.

overweight too heavy or fat. OPP
underweight.

base sth on sth use an idea, fact, etc. as the
point from which sth can be developed.

starchy food food containing a lot of
carbohydrates (see Word Focus).

wholemeal bread bread made with the
whole grains of wheat.

contain sth if one thing contains another,
it has that thing inside it or as part of it.

source where sth comes from.

full feeling you have had enough to eat.

fattening making you fat. OPP slimming.

calorie a measure of the energy you get
from food. (People who want to lose
weight often count calories.)

portion an amount of food for one person.

dairy products products made from milk,
e.g. cheese, butter.

obesity a condition in which sb is too fat
in a way that is not healthy. obese ADJ.

unfit not in good physical condition.
OPP fit.

brisk moving fast, especially on foot.

DIY ABBREV Do-It-Yourself doing home
repairs yourself instead of paying sb.

boost sth make sth increase. boost N.

coordination the ability to control your
movements well.

ensure sth make sure that sth happens.

minimum the smallest amount possible.
OPP maximum.

intense involving a lot of action or
concentration in a short period of time.

71

Weather conditions

I woke at **dawn** and poked my head out of the tent. The camp looked quite different in **daylight.** There had been a heavy **frost**, and it was **bitterly cold**. No wonder my feet were **freezing**.

We had a **torrential downpour** while I was out, and I got **soaked**. Then all of a sudden it stopped, the sun **came out**, and there was the most beautiful **rainbow**.

Well, it began to **cloud over** after breakfast, and we had a bit of **drizzle on and off** for most of the morning. Fortunately, it **cleared up** after lunch, but it still felt quite **chilly**.

We were **sweating** as soon as we got off the plane. It was absolutely **boiling** outside, and I've never been anywhere as **humid** as that.

When we left, there was a gentle **breeze** and the hills were hidden by the morning **mist** ▼. It was **mild**, but felt quite **damp**.

WORD FOCUS

Mist is a mass of small water drops in the air quite close to the ground, making it quite difficult to see. **misty** ADJ. Mist is similar to fog, but not as thick or as difficult to see through.

dawn the time in the morning when it starts to get light. OPP dusk.

daylight the light that comes from the sun during the day.

frost a thin layer of ice formed on the ground and other surfaces when the temperature falls below 0ºC. frosty ADJ.

bitterly cold very cold.

freezing very cold. OPP boiling.

torrential (of rain) very heavy.

downpour a large amount of rain that starts suddenly.

soaked extremely wet. SYN soaking wet.

come out (of the sun) start to appear.

rainbow an arc of colours in the sky when the sun shines while it is raining.

cloud over become cloudy.

drizzle light rain. drizzle V.

on and off/off and on sometimes, but not regularly or continuously.

clear up if the weather clears up, the clouds or rain go away.

chilly just too cold to feel comfortable.

sweat produce water on your skin when you are hot, nervous or ill. sweat N.

humid hot and wet in a way that makes you feel uncomfortable. humidity N.

breeze a light wind. breezy ADJ.

mild quite warm and pleasant; warmer than usual for a cold time of year.

damp slightly wet, often in an unpleasant way.

Climate change

Over the last 100 years, the average temperature of the earth's **surface** has risen by 0.74 degrees Celsius, with human activity now believed to be the **principal** cause of **global warming**▼. If **emissions** from **greenhouse gases**▼ continue to rise, the **impact** could be **devastating**. We will experience more extreme weather events such as **floods**, **hurricanes**, **prolonged heatwaves** and **drought**, and sea levels could rise even further.

In **the Arctic**, the temperature is rising twice as fast: sea ice is **melting** at an **alarming** rate, and this is already **threatening** the **existence** of many different **species**.

WORD FOCUS

Global warming is the increase in temperature of the earth's atmosphere that is caused by particular gases, especially **carbon dioxide** (CO_2). These gases are often referred to as **greenhouse gases**.

surface the top layer or outside part of sth: *a hard surface, the earth's surface.*

principal most important; main.

emission the action of letting a gas into the air (also the gas itself).

impact (of sth on sth/sb) the powerful effect that sth has on sth/sb.

devastating causing a lot of damage and destruction. **devastation** N.

flood a large amount of water that covers an area that was dry before.

hurricane a violent storm with extremely strong winds and heavy rain.

prolonged continuing for a long time.

heatwave a continuous period of very hot weather.

drought a long period of dry weather when there is little or no rain and crops die.

the Arctic the region that is the most northern part of the world. The most southern region is **the Antarctic**.

melt (sth) become liquid or make sth become liquid because of heating.

alarming causing worry and fear.

threaten sth be likely to harm or destroy sth. **threat** N.

existence the state of being a real or living thing. **exist** V.

species a plant or animal group whose members have similar features and are able to produce young plants or animals.

Natural disasters

Flood crisis deepens

After the worst **floods** in Pakistan for 80 years, affecting over 14 million people, the **crisis** has now deepened as further heavy rains **hamper** the **relief operation**. Helicopters, vital in the rescue of **stranded survivors,** are being **grounded** because of bad weather. These helicopters are essential because many of the bridges have been **swept away**, and they are the only way of reaching the many villages which have been **cut off** by the flood waters. The situation is particularly bad in the Swat Valley where there has been a series of new flood **alerts**. The government has already **evacuated** a million people, and many more are now **fleeing** the area. Meanwhile, aid is finally beginning to arrive. The **priorities** are food, clean drinking water, medicine and **shelter**. ●

WORD FOCUS

A **disaster** is a terrible event that causes a lot of damage or kills a lot of people. Examples of natural disasters include hurricanes, **earthquakes** (= a sudden shaking movement of the ground), and **tidal waves** (= a large ocean wave that destroys things when it reaches land).

flood a large amount of water covering an area of land that was dry before. flood (sth) v.

crisis an urgent, difficult or dangerous situation: *a political/economic crisis.*

hamper sth OFTEN PASSIVE prevent sth from happening or progressing normally.

relief operation the process of giving food, medicine, etc. to people who need help.

stranded left somewhere with no way of going anywhere else.

survivor sb who continues to live after an event that could have killed them. survive (sth) v, survival N.

ground sth OFTEN PASSIVE stop a plane from leaving the ground.

sweep sth away OFTEN PASSIVE completely remove sth suddenly with a lot of force.

cut sb/sth off OFTEN PASSIVE prevent sb/sth from leaving or reaching a place.

alert a warning of a problem or danger. (If you alert sb, you tell them of a possible danger.)

evacuate sb make sb leave a building or place because it is not safe. evacuation N.

flee (sth/from sth) PT fled PP fled escape from a dangerous situation.

priority sth important that must be done first or needs more attention than anything else.

shelter a place where people are protected from bad weather or danger. shelter v.

Animals

hump

camel

leopard

giraffe

stripes

zebra

wolf

chimpanzee
(chimp INF)

kangaroo

tail

gorilla

polar bear

shark

dolphin

seal

crocodile

swan

beak

eagle

wing

penguin

feathers

owl

parrot

79

Saving wildlife

Some **species** such as the western black **rhinoceros** have **died out** completely; others such as the **tiger** are increasingly **in danger of extinction**. And the main **threat to** all of this **wildlife** is destructive human activity, either directly through **unsustainable hunting** and fishing, or indirectly as a result of climate change and **deforestation**, both of which rob animals of their **natural habitat**. In the face of these dangers, we need a careful and **sustained** programme of **conservation** in order to **ensure** the **survival** of so many **vulnerable** and **endangered** animals.

tiger

panda

rhinoceros/rhino

species a plant or animal group whose
members have similar features and
are able to produce young plants or
animals.

die out become weaker or less common
and then disappear completely.

extinction the situation when a plant
or animal group no longer exists: *in
danger of extinction*. extinct ADJ.

threat (to sth) a situation or activity that
could cause harm or danger to sth.

wildlife the animals, birds and plants that
live in natural conditions.

unsustainable not capable of continuing
at the same rate, level, etc.

hunting the activity of chasing and killing
wild animals. hunt (sth) v.

deforestation the process of removing
trees from an area of land.

natural habitat the type of place where an
animal usually lives or a plant usually
grows.

sustained continuing at the same level for
a long time.

conservation the protection of natural
things, e.g. animals, plants or forests, to
stop them being damaged or destroyed.

ensure sth make certain that sth happens.

survival the state of continuing to live or
exist. survive (sth) v.

vulnerable weak and easily hurt.

endangered becoming less common
and in danger of disappearing from
the world.

Types of building

detached house	a house which stands alone and is not joined to another. A semi-detached house is joined to another house by one wall that they share.
terraced house	a house in a row of similar houses, joined together on both sides.
bungalow	a house built on one level with no stairs.
villa	**1** a large house with a garden in a warm country, often used for holidays. **2** an elegant town house.
cottage	a small house, especially in the country.
shed	a small building, usually made of wood, in which you store (= keep) things.
barn	a large building on a farm where animals, crops or machinery are kept.
stable	a building where horses are kept.
greenhouse	a building with glass sides and a glass roof where plants are grown.
nursing home	a building where elderly people live and are cared for.

warehouse	a commercial building used for storage (= storing/keeping goods).
town hall	a building containing local government offices, and in Britain, usually a hall for public meetings, concerts, etc.
multi-storey car park	a large building with several floors for parking cars in.
mall/shopping mall	a large building or covered area that has many shops, restaurants, etc. in it.
service station	1 a place where you buy petrol, oil, etc. for a vehicle. SYN petrol station. 2 a place beside a motorway where petrol, food, and toilets are available.
shelter	a building or an area with a roof over it which protects you from bad weather or danger.
high-rise building	a tall building of offices or flats. (An extremely tall building is a skyscraper.)
monument	a building, column, etc. built to remind people of a famous person or event.
premises	the buildings and surrounding land that a business owns or uses.
derelict building	a building which is empty, not used and in very bad condition.

Ancient buildings

Situated at Baalbek, 53 miles from Beirut, **stand** ▼ the **ruins** of a group of Roman **temples constructed** in the first century A.D. **Surrounding** the temples is a massive **stone** wall, and at one end **sit** ▼ three of the largest cut **blocks** of stone in the world. The largest of these weighs about 800 **tons**. This block would have been **transported** from a **quarry** almost a mile away, and possibly lifted about seven metres into position. Few modern industrial **cranes** would be capable of lifting the blocks.

The Roman **arch** is one of the greatest **inventions** in architecture. Arches **enabled** the Romans to create very large buildings with simple materials, and to build and **support** bridges, **aqueducts,** temples and palaces. Later **civilizations** have used arches in building cathedrals, **doorways** and windows. Their purpose is not only **structural** but **aesthetic.**

WORD FOCUS

Stand, lie and **sit** are often used when describing the position of sth.
The house stands on top of a hill.
The stones sit next to the monument.
The village lies next to the river.

ruins the parts of a building that remain after it has been badly damaged.

temple a building used for worship in some religions, e.g. Buddhism and Hinduism.

construct sth build sth.

surround sth be all around sth.

stone a hard, natural substance found in the ground which is used for building.

block a large piece of solid material.

ton a unit of weight, approx 1,000 kilos.

transport sth take sth to another place.

quarry a place where large amounts of stone are taken out of the ground.

crane a tall machine with a long arm, used to lift and move building materials.

arch a curved structure that supports the weight of sth, e.g. a bridge.

invention sth that has been designed which has not existed before.
invent sth v.

enable sb to do sth make it possible for sb to do sth.

support sth hold sth in position.

aqueduct a structure like a bridge that takes water across a valley.

civilization a society that has developed its own culture and institutions.

doorway an opening into a building or room.

structural connected with the way in which sth is built. **structure** N.

aesthetic concerned with beauty and the understanding of beautiful things.

Describing a building

The Hotel Regis is a four-star hotel which can **accommodate** about 80 guests. Located high up in a magnificent **setting**, the hotel **overlooks** the city below and is a well-known **landmark**.

As you **approach** the hotel along the tree-lined **drive**, you begin to see the **imposing exterior** with its elegant **columns** on either side of the entrance. The **design** is pure, classical elegance.

Entering the **lobby**, you cannot fail to be impressed by the **marble** floors and **pillars** throughout. To one side, there is a large reception area with two lifts, and in front of you is a **fine staircase leading to** the bedrooms and the Presidential **Suite**. To the right, a **corridor** leads to an **internal courtyard** full of tropical plants, and at the rear there is a magnificent **terrace** with gardens. The **basement** area **consists of** a spa and treatment rooms.

column SYN **pillar**

accommodate sb provide sb with a room or place to sleep, live, etc.

setting the position where sth is and its surroundings.

overlook sth have a view of sth from above.

landmark a famous building or object that you can see and recognize easily.

approach sth move closer to sth.

drive/driveway a wide path for a car, leading to an entrance.

imposing large and impressive.

exterior the outside of a building.

design the way in which sth is planned and made. design sth v.

lobby the area inside the entrance to a hotel, theatre, etc.

marble a hard, smooth stone used in building and for making statues.

fine of very good quality.

staircase a set of stairs inside a building.

lead to sth go to a particular place.

suite a set of connected rooms in a hotel.

corridor a long, narrow passage in a building.

internal existing inside a building.

courtyard an open space that is surrounded by walls or buildings.

terrace a flat outdoor area next to a building where you can sit outside to eat, relax, etc.

basement a room or floor below the ground floor.

consist of sth be formed or made up of sth.

Building work

recommendabuilder.com

JACKO Can anyone recommend a good building company in Edinburgh?

LOUIE *Design Works* **demolished** the wall to the **rear** of my house as requested, and **removed** all the **debris** from the **site**. They were punctual and tidy. No complaints!

ANNIE We used *SJ Construction* to **insulate** our **loft**. They were excellent.

MEG *Melrose Builders* **extended** my **existing** kitchen to create a large kitchen-dining area. They completed the job to a high **standard**.

ALI We needed to **strengthen** the roof structure and **tile** it. *David Beeton and Son* gave us a reasonable **quote**, and the work was done on time.

ROB *Solars For You* installed **solar panels** on our roof and connected them to the hot water supply. The work was done on time, but some of it was rather **shoddy**.

AILSA We used *Pritchard and Co* to **convert** the garage **into** a guest room and **fit** a new bathroom. I was very satisfied with their **workmanship**.

demolish sth pull down a wall, building, etc.

rear the back of sth.

remove sth take sth away from a place.

debris the broken pieces that are left when sth has been destroyed.

site an area of land where sth is being built: *building site*.

insulate sth cover sth with a material that stops heat, cold, etc. passing through.

loft a space just below a roof which is used to store things.

extend sth make sth longer or larger.

existing used to describe sth that is there now, but might be changed or replaced.

standard a level of quality that people consider acceptable: *a high standard*.

strengthen sth make sth stronger.

tile sth cover sth with tiles (= pieces of baked clay used for covering roofs or floors).

quote INF a statement of how much a particular piece of work will cost.

install sth fix equipment into position: *install a phone line/central heating*.

solar panel a piece of equipment that uses energy from the sun to produce power.

shoddy done badly and carelessly.

convert sth into sth change sth from one purpose or form into another. conversion N.

fit sth put or fix sth into the correct position: *fit a bathroom/carpet*.

workmanship the skill with which sb makes or does sth.

8.5 Impressive buildings

What makes a building impressive?

brick

'For me, the choice of **building materials** is very important–**brick**, stone, glass or **concrete**–and whether for example they are **shiny** or **solid**.'

'As with classical **architecture**, I **appreciate** balance and **symmetry** in buildings.'

'A beautiful building should create an **atmosphere** which raises your **spirits** and makes you **long** to be there.'

'I'm a musician, so for me, good **acoustics** are essential. Many concert halls are **purpose-built**, so I appreciate a simple **functional** building that works.'

'I particularly like to see **graceful** lines, and I prefer **open plan** spaces which make buildings more **versatile**.'

'In architecture, I look for **originality** in building design, and I'm interested in **innovative** construction **techniques**. I love buildings that break the rules and surprise me. It's important how they look alongside the existing buildings.'

building material a substance that buildings can be made from, e.g. stone.

concrete building material made by mixing sand, cement, stones and water.

shiny smooth and bright.

solid hard or firm.

architecture the art or study of designing buildings. (The designer is an architect.)

appreciate sth recognize how good or useful sth is. appreciation N.

symmetry the quality of having two halves that are exactly the same, and balance each other perfectly.

atmosphere the feeling or mood that exists in a particular place.

spirits sb's feeling or state of mind.

long to do sth want sth very much.

acoustics the way sound is heard in a room, as a result of its shape and size.

purpose-built designed and built for one particular purpose.

functional having a simple, effective design.

graceful elegant in form and movement.

open plan an open plan area does not have inside walls dividing it up into rooms.

versatile able to be used in many different ways.

originality the quality of being new and different from anything created before.

innovative new, unusual and advanced.

technique a way of doing sth using a special skill.

Computer hardware

WORD FOCUS

Hardware refers to the physical and electronic parts of a computer (see pictures.) **Software** refers to the programs you use to make the computer do different things: *system software*.
You **install** a new piece of software onto the **hard drive** (= the part of the computer that reads data) and then **run** it (= start the program).

1 PC = Personal computer
2 monitor
3 screen
4 webcam
5 keyboard
6 keys
7 escape key
8 space bar
9 return (key)
10 DVD drive
11 CD-ROMs
12 USB port
13 flashdrive
   SYN memory stick
14 mouse
15 headset
16 microphone
17 printer

93

Word processing

A: Show me how to type a **document**.

B: It's easy! Just **click on** this **icon**. It will open a document and you can start **typing**.

A: Suppose I make a mistake?

B: Just press the **delete button.** And it's easy to move **text** around on the page: you can **cut** a sentence or paragraph and **paste** it in a different place. Don't forget that you can also correct your spelling by using the **spellchecker.**

A: Then do I just **close** the document?

B: No, you have to **save** it. You click on the 'save' icon, and put it in a **folder**.

A: How about making a paper copy?

B: Just **pull down** this **menu**, and click on 'print'. It will **print out** your document for you. And remember to **back up** your work when you finish.

icons

cut   paste

save   print

document a piece of text
produced electronically
on a computer.

click on sth place the cursor (= the mark
on the screen which shows where you
are working) over sth and press on the
mouse.

type sth write sth using a keyboard.

delete button a key you press to remove
sth from the computer's memory.

text a piece of written material (in this
case, in your document).

spellchecker a computer program that
will tell you if your spelling is correct.

close sth stop sth operating so that it
disappears from your screen.

folder a group of
programs or
documents stored
in a computer.

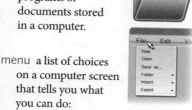

menu a list of choices
on a computer screen
that tells you what
you can do:
pull down a menu.

print sth out produce a paper copy of a
document from a computer. printout N.

back sth up make a copy of information
on your computer. backup copy N.

Business emails

Useful **etiquette** for replies to emails

- ✉ Keep emails **concise**; **respond** quickly.
- ✉ Do not use email for **confidential** information.
- ✉ Do not write in **upper case**; it looks as if you are shouting.
- ✉ Do not use **emoticons** or **abbreviations** such as **LOL.**
- ✉ Do not **forward** silly jokes to business contacts, or reply to **spam.**
- ✉ Do not **attach** unnecessary **files.**
- ✉ Use the **Bcc box** when replying to a group of people. This means that you won't be **publicizing** people's email addresses without their permission.
- ✉ Do not **delete** the **sender's** email. Keep the message **thread** by clicking on the **reply** button, and not 'new mail'. This will save the **recipient** time.

etiquette the rules of correct or polite behaviour. On the internet, this is often called netiquette (= net etiquette).

concise giving only the information which is important, using few words.

respond to sb/sth reply to sb/sth. response N.

confidential meant to be kept secret and not shared with other people.

upper case = A, B, C, rather than a, b, c. SYN capital letters. OPP lower case.

emoticon a special keyboard symbol which shows the sender's feelings, e.g. ☺, ☹.

abbreviation the short form of words or phrases, e.g. LOL = laughing out loud.

forward sth (to sb) send an email, letter or parcel that you have received on to another address.

spam unwanted emails sent to a large number of people. SYN junk mail.

attach sth send a document, picture, etc. with an email. attachment N.

file a set of data on a computer.

publicize sth make sth known to the public. publicity N.

delete sth remove sth that has been stored or written on a computer.

sender a person who sends sth, e.g. an email, a parcel. OPP recipient.

thread a series of connected email messages about a particular subject.

Internet terms

log on/log in	perform the actions that let you start to use the computer. OPP log off/log out.
broadband	a type of connection to the internet that allows you to receive or send a lot of information very quickly: *broadband speed*.
cyberspace ▶	the imaginary place where electronic messages exist while they are being sent between computers.
virtual	using computer sounds and images which make you feel as if an imagined situation is real: *virtual reality, virtual community*.
bookmark	a record of the address of a website that allows you to find it easily again. bookmark sth v.
download sth	move data from another computer or the internet onto your computer. OPP upload sth. download n.

webcast	message, talk, etc. happening now on the internet; also a live broadcast.
window	one of the different work areas on a computer screen.
search engine	a computer program used for looking for information on the internet, e.g. Google, AOL.
hit	a visit by someone to a particular website: *We've had 1000 hits on our site.*
hyperlink	a word or an image in a computer document that you can click on in order to move to a related document or image. This is often called a link.
crash	If a computer crashes, it stops working suddenly.
hacker	sb who connects to your computer, secretly and often illegally, and looks at or changes information on your system. hack into sth v.

WORD FOCUS

Cyber-, *virtual* and *web-* are often combined with other words to refer to the use of the internet, e.g. *cyber crime*, *cyber-bully*; *virtual games*, *virtual worlds*; *web page*, *website*.

9.5

Using the internet

What do you use the internet for?

'I do a lot of online shopping–particularly on **auction** sites like *ebay*. It's astonishing how **e-commerce** ▼ has **taken off** in recent years.'

'I use it to **keep in touch**–email, **chat rooms, message boards**, etc. Plus I **surf** the internet for **instructional video clips, tutorials**, and things like that for my hobbies–cookery and painting.'

'I'm a student, so I need **access to** academic information. You can **do a search** on any topic–you just **google** it and find masses of stuff. And I spend a lot of time **browsing** music sites and playing **interactive** games.'

'I like to keep **up-to-date** by reading the newspapers and magazines online. I also follow various **blogs** about political issues.'

'I'm doing a **web-based** training course, which is great. It's really **flexible**–I can do it where and when I like.'

WORD FOCUS

The prefix **e-** (meaning 'electronic') is often used in words related to the internet, e.g. **e-book** (= electronic book), **e-commerce**, **e-banking**.

auction a public event where things are sold to people who offer the most money for them.

take off become successful or popular very quickly or suddenly.

keep in touch (with sb) stay in contact with sb by writing, emailing, phoning, etc.

chat room an area on the internet where people can communicate with each other.

message board a place on a website where you can write or read messages.

surf (the internet) use the internet.

instructional teaching people sth.

video clip a short digital film that can be seen on a website such as *YouTube*.

tutorial a film or set of instructions on the internet that tells you how to do sth.

access (to sth) the opportunity or right to have, see or use sth.

do a search look for information about sth on the internet. SYN google sth.

browse (the internet) look in a relaxed way at a number of sites on the internet.

interactive an interactive game reacts to the information or instructions you give it.

up-to-date having the most recent information. OPP out-of-date.

blog a website where sb writes regularly about events or topics of interest. (The person who writes blogs is a blogger.)

web-based happening on the internet.

flexible able to make changes or deal with a situation that is changing. OPP inflexible.

9.6 Social networking

Social networking sites such as *Facebook* and *MySpace* allow people to **interact with** each other, **share** photos, find friends and make **contacts**. Many businesses with websites also provide a clickable **link** to a Facebook page.

If you decide to **sign up to** one of these sites, you go to the **home page** and **enter** certain pieces of personal **data**, including your name, email address and a **password**. You are then able to create a **profile**. You can include whatever **biodata** you like, and also **upload** a profile picture.

Now you are ready to find your friends on the site; you do this using your email **address book**. You send them a friends' request, and once they have **approved** you, you can **access** each other's profile, read their **posts ▼**, see their photos and videos, etc. You can also **specify** which parts of your profile you will allow people to see by clicking the **privacy button**.

WORD FOCUS

A **post** or **posting** is a message you leave on a website. The verb is **post**:
I posted a question on the website.
100 jobs are posted every week.

social networking site a website that allows you to communicate with friends and make new friends.

interact with sb (of two or more people) communicate with and react to each other.

share sth show or tell sb sth.

contact a person you know or meet on a social networking site.

link a connection between electronic documents or areas on the internet.

sign up (to sth) agree to join sth.

home page the main page on a website.

enter sth write sth on a computer.

data information or facts about sb/sth.

password secret numbers or letters you enter to be able to use a system or website.

profile a description of sb.

biodata information about you and what you have done in your life.

upload sth move data from a smaller computer system to a large one.

address book a computer file where you store email and internet addresses.

approve sb agree that sb is acceptable.

access sth (of computing) open a file to get information.

specify sth state sth clearly or choose sth.

privacy a state in which you can do things without other people knowing what you are doing.

button a symbol on a computer screen.

9.7

Mobile phones

What problems do you have?

'Phones have to do so much these days: they're basically a **hard drive** with a screen; they're a communication **device**, and they've also got a camera, a **music player**, and so on. It's not surprising they get **bugs** or **go wrong**.'

'It's annoying that the **reception** in my area is so poor; it's hard to get a **signal**.'

'My phone is **pay-as-you-go** ▼, and I'm always **running out of credit** ▼. I keep forgetting to **top it up**.'

'My phone's old, so I have to **charge it up** all the time; the **battery's** no good. I really need to **upgrade**.'

'I do a lot of **texting**, but most **texts** I send to one friend don't arrive, and I can't receive texts from her either.'

'My phone **goes off**, but there's no one there. I've tried removing the **SIM card** and putting it back, but it doesn't help.'

WORD FOCUS

When you buy a mobile phone, you can have a **contract**, i.e. you pay a monthly bill, or use **pay-as-you-go**, i.e. before you make the calls, you buy a fixed amount of time (= **credit**). SYN **prepaid**.

---

hard drive the part of a computer that stores data and programs.

device a piece of equipment which has been designed to do a particular job.

music player a program on a mobile or MP3 player that plays music.

bug a fault in a computer system, mobile phone, etc.

go wrong stop working correctly.

reception the quality of radio, TV and phone signals that are broadcast or transmitted.

signal electrical waves carrying sound, pictures, etc. to a mobile phone, TV, etc.

run out of sth If you run out of credit on your mobile phone, you have no money left in your phone account.

top up (your phone) = pay more money so that you can make more calls.

charge sth (up) pass electricity through sth so that it is stored there.

battery a device in a clock, mobile phone, etc. which produces the electricity that makes it work.

upgrade (sth) get a more powerful or up-to-date phone, computer, etc. upgrade N.

texting sending and receiving written messages (= texts) on a mobile phone. text sb V.

go off (of a phone, an alarm, etc.) start to ring, buzz, vibrate, etc.

SIM card a memory card in a mobile phone.

10.1 The Scientific Method

The Scientific Method is a **logical** and **rational** order of steps by which scientists reach **conclusions** about the world around them. These steps are:

Observation: this is a research **phase.** You **gather** information from as many **sources** as possible.

Hypothesis ▼: this is a simple **statement** defining what you think the **outcome** of your experiment will be. It could be described as **an educated guess**.

Experiment: this tests whether your hypothesis is true or false. You must ensure that it is a **fair** test by changing only one **factor** at a time.

Analysis and conclusion: once the experiment is complete, collect your **measurements** and **analyse** them to see if your hypothesis is true or false. If it is false, you need to **construct** a new hypothesis, starting the **process** again.

WORD FOCUS

A **hypothesis** is an idea that you suggest as the explanation for something, but which has not yet been proven to be true or correct. SYN **theory**; **hypothetical** ADJ. You can **formulate** (= create) **a hypothesis** or **confirm it** (= show it is true or correct).

logical following the rules of logic, in which ideas are based on things that are known to work or be true. OPP illogical.

rational based on reason and not emotions. OPP irrational.

conclusion sth you decide after thinking about it carefully: *reach a conclusion*.

observation the process of watching sb/sth carefully in order to learn sth. observe sth v.

phase a stage in a process of change or development.

gather sth bring together things or facts that you have found in different places.

source a person, book or document that provides information.

statement sth you write or say that gives information or an opinion.

outcome the result or effect of sth.

an educated guess a guess that is probably correct because it is based on knowledge.

experiment a scientific test done to find out if a particular idea is true. experiment v.

fair honest, acceptable and appropriate.

factor one of several things that influence or cause a situation.

analysis a careful examination of sth in order to understand it better. analyse sth v.

measurement the size, degree, or quantity of sth, found after careful examination.

construct sth create an idea or system.

process a method of doing or making sth.

Gravity

Gravity is the **force** that **draws** an object or a living thing **downwards.** We say that things which are pulled by gravity have **mass.**

Things that are falling still have mass, but we cannot **calculate** their weight, so we say that they are **weightless. Astronauts** and **spacecraft ▼** in **outer space** can be weightless; they appear to be **floating.** In fact, they are falling in an **orbit** around the Earth. In order to move, spacecrafts need **rockets ▼**, and astronauts use their arms or legs to jump or stop.

Sir Isaac Newton **discovered** gravity when he saw an apple fall from a tree; his rules are simple but surprisingly **accurate.** Albert Einstein showed that gravity could be explained as the **bending** of space and time by mass. He **predicted** that time slows down near a large mass, and this has been **verified** using very accurate clocks on satellites.

WORD FOCUS

A **spacecraft** is a vehicle that travels in space. A **rocket** is a vehicle shaped like a tube that travels in space and provides the power for a spacecraft. When a rocket is sent up into space, we say it has been **launched**.

gravity the force that attracts objects in space towards each other, and that on earth pulls them towards the ground.

force PHYSICS an effect that causes things to move in a particular way.

draw sth move sth by pulling it gently.

downwards towards the ground or towards a lower level. OPP upwards.

mass TECHNICAL the quantity of material that sth contains. SYN weight NON-TECHNICAL.

calculate sth discover a number or amount using maths. calculation N.

weightless having no weight, especially because of being outside the Earth's atmosphere. weightlessness N.

astronaut sb who travels and works in space.

outer space (also space) the area outside the Earth's atmosphere where all the other planets and stars are.

float move slowly in the air or on water.

orbit a curved path followed by a planet or a spacecraft as it moves around a star or planet. orbit (around) sth V.

discover sth be the first person to become aware that a particular thing or place exists. discovery N.

accurate correct and true in every detail.

bend sth change the direction of sth to form a curve (= a shape like part of a circle).

predict sth say sth will happen in the future.

verify sth check or prove that sth is correct or true.

BASIC SCIENCE

10.3

Biology quiz

True or False? See answers on page 377.

1. **Biology** is the **scientific** study of the life and structure of plants and animals. ☐

2. The **oxygen** we breathe comes from plants and the ocean. ☐

3. **Bacteria** have leaves and **roots**. ☐

4. The basic **unit** of all living **organisms** is the cell. ☐

5. The **nucleus** is a structure within each cell that contains **genetic** ▼ information, or **DNA** ▼. ☐

6. The **stem** of a plant is below ground. ☐

7. The human **skeleton** consists of 106 **bones**. ☐

8. An elephant is a **marine mammal.** ☐

9. A **clone** is any cell that is **genetically** ▼ identical to another. ☐

10. An **embryo** is a young animal or plant in the early stages of development after birth. ☐

WORD FOCUS

A **gene** is a chemical unit within the nucleus of a cell that carries particular characteristics to a living thing from its parents. **genetic** ADJ, **genetically** ADV. Genes are linked together in long strands of material called **DNA** (deoxyribonucleic acid).

biology the scientific study of living things.
scientific relating to science (= the study
    of the structure and behaviour of
    natural things).
oxygen (= O$_2$) a gas in the air that we
    breathe.
bacteria PL N simple, tiny forms of life
    consisting of a single cell with no
    nucleus. bacterial ADJ.
root the part of a plant that grows under
    the ground, and takes in water and
    minerals.
unit a single, individual thing that is part
    of something larger.
organism a living thing, especially one
    that is extremely small.
cell the smallest unit of living matter that
    can exist alone.
nucleus the middle part of a cell.
stem the long, thin part of a plant above
    the ground, from which leaves grow.
skeleton the set of bones (see below) that
    supports a human or animal body.
bone any of the hard structural parts of a
    human or animal.
marine connected with the sea.
mammal any animal that gives birth to live
    babies, not eggs, and feeds them on milk.
clone an exact copy of a plant or animal
    created in a laboratory.
identical exactly the same.
embryo a young animal or plant in
    the very early stages of development
    before birth.

10.4 Chemistry in cooking

Yeast is a **substance** which is essential for bread-making. It is a **microscopic** organism which is in fact a kind of **fungus**. When you mix it with bread **dough**, it **converts** the sugars in the dough into **carbon dioxide**. This makes the dough **expand** as the gas forms **bubbles**. When the bread is baked, the yeast dies, and the pockets of air **set**, making the bread soft and **spongy**.

In fact, cooking is really a series of **chemical reactions**. Green vegetables, for example, become brighter when **plunged** in boiling water; this is because heat **forces** the **gases** surrounding the vegetable cells to expand and escape. As a result, you can see the green **pigment** more clearly. However, longer cooking makes the plant's cell walls **shrink** and **release** an **acid** ▼, and as a result, the colour **fades**.

WORD FOCUS

In chemistry, an **acid** is a chemical substance with a **ph value** (= a measure in chemistry) of less than seven: *sulphuric/nitric acid*. Strong acids can damage your skin. A substance with a ph value of more than seven is an **alkali**.

yeast a substance that makes bread rise.

substance a particular type of solid, gas, or liquid.

microscopic so small that it can only be seen through a microscope (= a special instrument).

fungus a type of living thing that lives on dead plants, e.g. mushrooms.

dough a mixture of flour and water that is made into bread and pastry.

convert sth into sth change sth from one form to another.

carbon dioxide (= CO_2) the gas produced when people and animals breathe out.

expand become larger in size or amount.

bubble a ball of air or gas in a liquid or solid substance.

set become hard and solid.

spongy soft and full of holes that contain air.

chemical connected with chemistry.

reaction a chemical change that happens when two or more substances are mixed.

plunge sth in/into sth push sth firmly and deeply into sth else.

force sth make sth happen or change.

gas a substance such as air which is not solid or liquid, and cannot usually be seen.

pigment a natural substance that makes plants, skin, hair, etc. a particular colour.

shrink become smaller.

release sth let a substance come out.

fade lose colour and brightness.

10.5

The science of sleep

What is sleep for?

Why do we sleep? This question has **baffled** scientists for centuries, and is still **unsolved**. One fact is certain: the **consequences** of sleep **deprivation** are very serious indeed, and are said to have been a possible factor in international disasters such as Chernobyl and the Exxon Valdez oil spill.

However, we do know that sleep is not a **passive** event but an **active** process, involving **physiological** changes in the body. It occurs in a **recurring cycle** of 90-110 minutes. During the first stage ('light sleep'), **muscle** activity slows down and slight **twitching** can occur. In stage two, the breathing **pattern** and heart rate slow down. In stage three, the brain begins to produce 'delta **waves**', which are large and slow, with breathing and heart rate **declining** further. The final stage of sleep is **characterized** by REM (Rapid Eye Movement): the brain is very active, and this is when dreaming occurs. Our eyes move around quickly (the **function** of this is unknown), and our bodies are effectively **paralyzed**, perhaps so that we do not try to **act out** our dreams. ●

baffle sb if sth baffles you, you cannot understand it or explain it.

unsolved is sth is unsolved, the correct answer or explanation has not been found.

consequence a result of sth that has happened.

deprivation when you do not have sth that you need in order to be healthy, comfortable or happy. **deprive sb of sth** v.

passive letting things happen to you without taking action. OPP active.

physiological connected with the way that the body of a living thing operates.

recurring happening again, several times. **recur** v.

cycle a series of events that happen again and again in the same order.

muscle a piece of body tissue that you relax or stretch to move your arms, legs, etc.

twitching sudden, small movements.

pattern the regular way sth happens, develops or is done.

wave the form that some kinds of energy, e.g. light or heat, take as they move.

decline become smaller, weaker, etc.

characterize sth be typical of sth.

function the job that sth is designed to do.

paralyze sb make sb lose the ability to move their body or part of it.

act sth out express your feelings through your behaviour or actions.

Chilean rescue

Chilean miners all saved

capsule

After being **trapped** underground for a **record** period of time, 33 **miners** were all **rescued** safely in an **operation** that lasted almost two days. The men were trapped on 5 August 2010, after a section of the *San José* **copper** mine in North Chile **collapsed**. Initially few thought they could **survive**, but 17 days later, **rescuers** discovered that the men were all still alive. They had gone to a secure room called a 'refuge' and had spent days listening to the sound of the **drills** above them. Finally, after 69 days underground, the men were **winched** to safety, one at a time, in a small **capsule** just 54 cm in **diameter**. There were enormous **cheers** each time another miner came up safely. Every single one was viewed as a **hero**, and most families from this religious community believed it was a **miracle**. ∎

trap sb OFTEN PASSIVE keep sb in a dangerous place or bad situation that they want to get away from but cannot.

record the highest or lowest amount or level that has ever been reached.

miner sb who works down a mine (= a deep hole under the ground where you find coal, gold, etc.).

rescue sb/sth save sb/sth from a dangerous or harmful situation. (People who do this are rescuers.) rescue N.

operation an organized activity involving different people doing different things.

copper (= Cu) a soft, reddish-brown metal used to make electrical wires, pipes, etc.

collapse fall down or fall in suddenly.

survive continue to live or exist despite being in a dangerous situation. survival N.

drill a tool or machine with a pointed end that is rotated to make holes.

winch sb (up) lift sb up in the air using a winch (= a machine for lifting heavy objects using a rope or chain).

diameter the measurement of a straight line passing from one side of a circle to the other, through the centre.

cheer a shout of joy or approval. cheer v.

hero sb who is admired for doing sth brave or good. (A woman is also called a heroine.)

miracle an act or event that does not follow the laws of nature and is believed to be caused by God.

Emergency landing

Miraculous escape

A US Airways plane has crashed into New York's Hudson River, but all 155 on board made a **miraculous** escape as the freezing waters rose around them.

Initial reports say the aircraft lost power in both engines shortly after take-off when a **flock** of birds flew into the plane. This has not been **confirmed**, but the plane began to **dip** coming towards the George Washington Bridge while people on the ground watched **in horror**. Passenger Alberto Panero takes up the story. "The plane **shook** a bit and immediately you could smell smoke and fire," he said. "**All of a sudden**, the captain came on and said '**Brace yourself** for **impact**,' and that's when we knew we were going into the water." The plane made an **extraordinary crash landing**, but managed to remain **intact**, so passengers were able to walk out onto the **wings**. In **sub**-zero temperatures, the **shivering** passengers were saved, **thanks to** the **swift** action taken by the fire **crews** and watching ferry crews on the river. Speaking of the **incident** later, Gov. David Paterson said, "I believe we've had a **miracle** on the Hudson." ●

miraculous completely unexpected and very lucky; like a miracle N. (see p.117)

initial happening at the beginning, or when you first see or hear about sth.

flock (of sth) a group of birds or sheep.

confirm sth state or show that sth is definitely true or correct. confirmation N.

dip go downwards or to a lower level.

in horror with a feeling of shock or fear.

shake move from side to side or up and down with quick short movements.

all of a sudden quickly and unexpectedly.

brace yourself (for sth) hold your body firm in preparation for violent movement.

impact the forceful effect of one object hitting another.

extraordinary very unusual.

crash landing an occasion when a plane has to land in a sudden and dangerous way.

intact complete and not damaged.

wing (of a plane) one of the flat parts on either side which help to keep it in the air.

sub- PREFIX below; less than: *sub-zero temperatures, substandard.*

shiver (of a person) shake slightly because you are cold, or ill.

thanks to sb/sth used to say that sth has happened because of sb/sth.

swift happening or done quickly.

crew a group of people with a particular skill who work together.

incident an unnatural or unpleasant event.

Oil spill

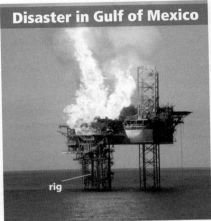

Disaster in Gulf of Mexico

rig

In April 2010, an **explosion** and fire on the Deepwater Horizon **rig** resulted in the death of eleven oil workers and a **catastrophic** oil **spill** into the Gulf of Mexico. Early attempts to **cap** the **well** all proved unsuccessful, and it was five months before scientists and engineers finally stopped the **leak** by **pumping** heavy **mud** into the top of the well from a ship. During that time it is **estimated** that almost five million **barrels** of oil **leaked** into the Gulf. At the same time, BP announced that the **clean-up operation** and **compensation** for **victims** could cost the company up to 40 **billion** dollars.

explosion a sudden, loud and violent
bursting open of sth, e.g. a bomb.
explode v.

catastrophic causing extreme damage
or making a lot of people suffer.
catastrophe N.

spill a spill happens when a liquid flows
over the edge of its container by
accident: *oil spill*. spill sth v.

cap sth put a cover or lid on sth.

well a deep hole made in the ground where
there is a supply of oil, gas or water.

leak the accidental passing of liquid or gas
through a small hole or crack. leak v.

pump sth make water, gas, air, etc. flow
in a particular direction using a pump
(= a machine that does this).

mud soft, wet earth.

estimate sth /ˈestɪmeɪt/ form an
approximate idea of the cost, size, value,
etc. of sth. estimate /ˈestɪmət/ N.

barrel 1 a unit in the oil industry between
120 and 159 litres. 2 a large round
container, usually made of wood or metal.

clean-up the process of removing
pollution, dirt, etc. from a place: *clean-up operation*.

compensation (for sth) sth, especially
money, that sb gives you because they
have hurt you, or damaged sth that
you own.

victim sb who suffers as a result of an
accident, a crime, disease, etc.

billion ABBREV BN 1,000,000,000.

121

Terrorist attack

Togo terrorist attack

It was football's worst **nightmare**, as details **emerged** last night of the **horrific** attack on the team bus carrying the Togo team to the Africa Nation's Cup in Angola. Striker Thomas Dossevi gave this **account**: 'We'd just crossed the border when we were **fired on** by **machine guns,** even though we were **surrounded by** police cars. It was clearly an **ambush.** When we felt the **bullets** hitting the bus, our **instincts** took over and everyone just hit the floor. We tried not to move, but two players were **shot** and there was blood everywhere.'

It should not have been a surprise. The Togo team had **ignored** advice not to travel by coach in a country where many roads are unsafe because of shootings, and **landmines** left from years of **bitter civil war.** This is now the second time a sports team has become the **target** for **terrorists** ▼: six policemen were killed when **gunmen opened fire** on the Sri Lankan cricket team bus in Lahore. ●

WORD FOCUS

Terrorists use violent action to achieve a political aim: *a terrorist attack*. **terrorism** N.

nightmare a very bad experience.

emerge (of facts, etc.) become known.

horrific very bad and shocking.

account a written or spoken report about sth that has happened.

fire (on sb) shoot bullets from a gun (at sb). fire N.

machine gun a gun that fires many bullets automatically one after another.

surround sb/sth OFTEN PASSIVE be all around or on all sides of sb/sth.

ambush a surprise attack by people waiting in a hidden position.

bullet a small metal object that is fired from a gun.

instinct a natural tendency that you are born with to behave in a particular way. instinctive ADJ.

shoot (sb) injure or kill sb using a gun.

ignore sth pay no attention to sth.

landmine a bomb hidden just under the ground that explodes when a person or vehicle moves over it.

bitter (of arguments, conflicts, etc.) very serious and unpleasant.

civil war fighting between different groups of people in the same country.

target a person, building or area that sb intends to attack.

gunman sb who uses a gun when fighting.

open fire start shooting a gun.

Jewellery raid

MOTORBIKE GANG RAID THE QUEEN'S JEWELLERS

Shopworkers experienced a **terrifying** moment when thieves **struck at** the Queen's jewellers. The **gang** on motorbikes **scared off passers-by**, then **smashed** the window of the Mappin & Webb store and **revved** their engines to **drown out** the noise of the glass as it **shattered**. They then reached inside and **grabbed** jewellery from a Rolex display. **Witnesses** in the **packed** street described the **raid** as being 'like a **gangster** film'. Petra Remias, who works opposite the store, said, 'People were just **staring** in **amazement**.'

Police have yet to **reveal** how much was taken and what the **goods** were worth.

terrifying extremely frightening.

strike (at) sth attack sth suddenly.

gang a group of criminals working together. (A **gangster** is a member of an organized group of criminals.)

scare sb off make sb so frightened that they run away.

passer-by sb who is walking past sth, especially when sth unexpected happens.

smash sth break sth noisily into many pieces by hitting it with force.

rev sth if you rev an engine, you press the accelerator to make the engine operate faster, and make more noise.

drown sth out stop a sound from being heard by making a louder noise.

shatter (sth) break or break sth suddenly into a lot of small pieces.

grab sth/sb suddenly or violently take hold of sth. SYN grab hold of sth.

witness sb who sees a crime or an accident. witness sth v.

packed very busy and full.

raid (on sth) an attack on a building, etc. in order to commit a crime.

stare (at sb/sth) look at sb/sth for a long time.

amazement a feeling of surprise or disbelief.

reveal sth let sth that is secret or unknown become known.

goods PL N objects produced for sale.

Forest fire

Russia declares emergency

A state of emergency was **declared** in seven regions yesterday as authorities struggled to **cope with** forest fires which have been **raging** for a week.

The fires, **prompted** by the prolonged **heatwave**, have **spread** at an **alarming** rate and have already **claimed** 34 lives, with thousands left **homeless**.

Firefighters have been struggling to **contain** about 600 **blazes** ▼, and President Dmitri Medvedev has now called on the armed forces to help **tackle** the fires.

Prime Minister Vladimir Putin visited one village where almost all the houses were **burned to the ground**. He tried to **reassure distraught** residents and **pledged** that their houses would all be rebuilt. Meanwhile, there are reports that a number of people have **drowned** in rivers and lakes after **seeking refuge** from the **intense** heat. ●

WORD FOCUS

A **blaze** is a very large and dangerous fire. A fire can **break out** (= start), or **die down** (= gradually become less strong), or somebody can **put it out** (= make it stop burning).

state of emergency a situation in which a government takes action to deal with an event that is putting lives in danger.

declare sth announce officially that sth is true or is happening.

cope with sth deal successfully with a difficult situation.

rage (of a fire, storm, etc.) continue with a lot of force.

prompt sth cause sth to happen.

heatwave a period of unusually hot weather.

spread cover a larger and larger area.

alarming causing worry and fear.

claim sth (of a disaster) cause sb's death.

homeless having no home.

contain sth stop sth harmful from spreading or getting worse.

tackle sth make an effort to deal with a difficult situation.

burn sth to the ground completely destroy sth by fire.

reassure sb do or say sth that makes sb less frightened or worried. **reassurance** N.

distraught extremely upset and anxious.

pledge sth formally promise to give or do sth. **pledge** N.

drown die because you have been underwater too long.

seek refuge look for shelter or protection from danger, trouble, etc.

intense very great or strong. SYN extreme.

Fruit

cherries

raspberries

blackberries

stone

plum

apricot

avocado

kiwi fruit

watermelon

Tropical fruit

mango

papaya

seeds

pomegranate

coconut

pineapple

fig

lychee

passion fruit

Vegetables

aubergine

courgette

leek

beetroot

cabbage

cauliflower

broccoli

fennel

celery

artichoke

asparagus

broad beans

beansprouts

parsnip

shallots (= like
small onions)

clove

garlic

corn on the cob
SYN sweetcorn

Salad

lettuce

cucumber

pepper

radish

spring onions

chicory

WORD FOCUS

A **salad** has **raw** (= uncooked) vegetables, and is often a **combination** (= two or more things put together) of different raw vegetables, which may be sliced or **grated** (= cut into very thin, small pieces).

Herbs and spices

Herbs

parsley

basil

thyme

rosemary

dill

mint

Spices

cinnamon

nutmeg

ginger

saffron

Meat

From a cow, we can eat steak, and the most expensive is fillet steak.

A young cow is called a calf, and the meat from a calf is called veal.

Some people also like offal. This refers to the organs of some animals that are eaten as food, e.g. liver or kidneys. Someone who doesn't eat meat is a vegetarian.

calf's liver

kidneys

In some countries, people also eat the meat from these birds and animals.

pheasant

turkey

duck

rabbit

goat

Fish and seafood

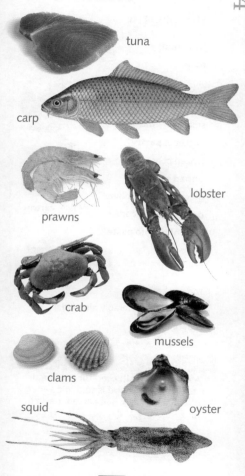

tuna

carp

prawns

lobster

crab

mussels

clams

oyster

squid

Different food

Shopping List

jar of **honey**

flour

jar

two **cartons** of orange juice

vinegar

small jar of **mustard**

packet of **pastry**

frozen peas

tinned salmon

green and black **olives**

decaffeinated coffee

carton

tube of tomato **paste**

tube

tomato **ketchup**

bag of **nuts** (preferably **almonds**)

loaf of bread

WORD FOCUS

A **container** is sth used for holding or storing things. Food is sold in a variety of containers, e.g. jar, carton, packet, tube, and bag.

honey the sweet, yellow substance, made by bees, often spread on bread.

flour a powder made from grain, and used to make bread, cakes, etc.

vinegar a liquid with a bitter taste, often added to oil and put on salads.

mustard a thick, cold yellow or brown sauce that is hot and spicy, often eaten with meat.

pastry a thick mixture of flour, fat and water, used to make tarts and pies.

frozen kept below the temperature at which water turns to ice.

tinned preserved in a tin/can. SYN canned.

salmon a large fish with pink flesh.

olive a small, sour green or black fruit that can be eaten or made into oil.

decaffeinated coffee = coffee that has had the caffeine removed from it.

paste a smooth mixture of tomato, fish, etc., that is put on bread or used in cooking.

ketchup a sweet, thick sauce made from tomatoes, and sold in jars or bottles.

nuts (see pictures)

almonds

peanuts

loaf of bread

Cooking

Potato **recipes**

For *Potato Dauphinoise*, **peel** and **slice** three or four large potatoes thinly, and arrange them in **layers** in a buttered dish. Add about a cup of cream and milk to the potatoes, **season** with salt and pepper, then cover with **grated** cheese. **Bake** in a **moderate** oven for an hour.

Potato Boulangere is quite similar. Add sliced onions to the sliced potato and use **stock** instead of cream and milk. Don't add cheese, but use some **rosemary** instead. **Chop** it **finely** and **scatter** it over the top of the potatoes. Cook for one hour.

For *roast* potatoes, **heat up** some oil or fat in a roasting tin. Meanwhile **boil** the potatoes for ten minutes, then **drain** and **shake** until they are completely dry. Add the potatoes to the hot oil or fat, return to the oven and cook for 45 minutes until they are really **crisp**.

recipe a set of cooking instructions.

peel sth remove the skin from sth. peel N.

slice sth cut sth into thin flat pieces. slice N.

layer a quantity or thickness of sth over a surface, or between two other things.

season sth add salt and pepper to sth.

grate sth rub food against a grater (see picture) to cut it into small pieces.

bake sth cook sth in the oven without oil/ fat (roast = cook in the oven with oil/ fat).

moderate neither very hot, good, large, etc., nor very cold, bad, small, etc.

stock water with the added flavour of meat, fish or vegetables.

rosemary a type of herb (see p.133).

chop sth cut sth into small pieces.

finely into very small pieces.

scatter sth (on/over/around sth) throw or drop things in different directions over an area.

heat sth up make sth hot.

boil sth cook sth in very hot water.

drain sth make sth dry or empty by removing all the liquid from it.

shake sth move sth quickly from side to side or up and down.

crisp pleasantly hard and dry.

grater

12.7

Describing food

What do I like? I like:

- oranges that are nice and **juicy** ▼
- **figs** that are really **ripe**
- meat that is **lean** and **tender**
- cheese that is **rich** and **creamy** ▼
- **raw** fish when it is very fresh
- **chilled** white wine
- curries that are quite **mild**
- chicken cooked on the **barbecue**
- **spicy** ▼ prawns
- **savoury** things rather than sweet things
- dark **bitter** chocolate
- the **aroma** of fresh coffee
- **sparkling** water rather than **still**.

What do I dislike? I don't like:

- **pickled** vegetables
- **smelly** cheese
- **overcooked** meat or vegetables
- food that is **bland** and **tasteless**.

WORD FOCUS

We can add –y to certain nouns to form adjectives meaning 'full of sth' or 'having a lot of sth':
salty = having a lot of salt.
spicy = having a lot of spice.
creamy = having a lot of cream.
juicy = full of juice.

barbecue

fig see picture page 129.

ripe ready to eat.

lean without any fat. OPP fatty.

tender (of meat) soft and easy to cut.
  OPP tough.

rich (of food) having a lot of fat, butter,
  eggs, etc.

raw not cooked.

chilled (of drinks) made cold in the fridge
  in order to be more pleasant.

mild (of flavour) not strong or spicy.

savoury having a taste that is salty, not
  sweet.

bitter a strong sharp taste that is not
  sweet. (It can be used positively or
  negatively.)

aroma a pleasant smell, often of food.

sparkling (of drinks) having bubbles of
  gas. SYN fizzy OPP still.

pickled preserved in vinegar.

smelly having an unpleasant smell.

overcooked cooked for too long. OPP
  undercooked.

bland not having a strong or interesting
  taste.

tasteless having little or no flavour.
  OPP tasty.

12.8

Dieting

How does dieting help?

Dieting ▼ doesn't mean you have to **starve**. In fact, you don't have to **give up** food you like – just **cut down on** certain things and change the way you eat. It does require **willpower**, but think of the **benefits**:

- With a **balanced diet** ▼, you will reduce your **calorie intake**, and the **vitamins** in your diet will produce improved health.

- With better health, your **metabolism** will speed up. This will give you more **energy**, and that means increased levels of activity and more weight loss.

- As you **lose weight** ▼, you take the **strain** off your heart that could otherwise lead to heart **disease** and **heart attacks**.

- You should feel better about your body. This leads to higher **self-esteem**.

WORD FOCUS

Your **diet** is the food you eat. A **balanced, healthy** or **varied diet** has the right food your body needs; a **bad diet** has the wrong food.
When people **diet** or **go on a diet**, they eat less in order to **lose weight**. OPP **put on weight**. We also use the noun **dieting**: *Dieting can help some people to lose weight.*

starve suffer or die because you don't have enough food. (In informal English we can also say, I'm starving = I'm very hungry.)

give sth up stop doing or having sth.

cut down on sth reduce the size, amount or number of sth.

willpower the ability to control your behaviour in order to achieve sth.

benefit an advantage or positive thing you get from a situation.

calorie a unit for measuring the energy you get from a food. (If you eat food with a high calorie content, you put on weight quickly.)

intake the amount of food, drink, etc. that you take into your body.

vitamin a natural substance found in food that keeps your body healthy. (Fruit and vegetables are high in vitamin C.)

metabolism the chemical process in your body that changes food into energy.

energy the amount of physical power you have to do an activity that requires effort. energetic ADJ.

strain the pressure that is put on your body when you are overweight or very active.

disease an illness, often serious, that affects an organ in your body.

heart attack a serious and sudden condition in which the heart stops working normally.

self-esteem a feeling of being confident in your own character and abilities.

13.1 High-street shopping

In Britain, the *high street* is often the main shopping street in the centre of town. Now, however, high streets all over the country are **in decline**. The popularity of **online shopping** has had a **devastating** effect on the high street, and most available money seems to be spent in large **out-of-town** shopping centres and developments. A few **upmarket retailers** are still prepared to **invest in affluent** ▼ middle-class towns, and clothes shops are able to **survive** because it seems that people still want to be able to try on clothes. But a large number of **chain stores**, selling well-known **brands**, are **closing down** and **going out of business**.

One of the things that angers retailers is that **consumers** still enjoy **window-shopping**, and will go in shops to get **expert** advice on a range of products. But **when it comes to** buying, they go home and buy at a different online store because it's cheaper. ●

WORD FOCUS

If you are **affluent**, you have plenty of money and a good standard of living. SYNS **wealthy, well off**. (**Well off** is often used in negative sentences, e.g. *He's not very well off.*)

in decline continuing to decrease in number, quality, value, etc.

online shopping the buying of goods on the internet.

devastating causing a lot of damage. SYN disastrous.

out-of-town located away from the centre of a town or city.

upmarket made for or used by people who have a lot of money. OPP downmarket.

retailer a person or business that sells goods to the public.

invest in sth put money into a business, property, etc. in the hope of making a profit.

survive continue to exist, especially in a difficult situation. survival N.

chain store one of a group of shops that all belong to the same company.

brand a type of product made by a particular company, e.g. *Ambre Solaire is a well-known brand of suntan lotion.*

close down (of a company) stop operating as a business. SYN go out of business.

consumer a person who buys goods or uses services.

window-shopping the activity of looking at goods in shop windows without buying anything.

expert having great knowledge or skill. A person who has this is an expert.

when it comes to sth/doing sth = when you are talking about sth/doing sth.

Street markets

stallholder

London Street Markets

stall

'If you're **after** **cut-price clothing**, you can **pick up** some real **bargains** at Petticoat Lane Market, especially if you're prepared to **haggle**.'

'Portobello Market sells **antiques**, **second-hand** clothing, and **bric-a-brac**. It **does a roaring trade** on Saturdays, but it's mainly **geared towards** tourists, and some of the prices are a **rip-off**.'

'I love the **hustle and bustle** of Camden Lock. They've got **loads of** ▼ stuff there, and it's good for me because I'm really **into vintage** clothes. Some of the antiques can be a bit **pricey**, though.'

'Shepherd's Bush Market is a nice local market for **ethnic** foods, clothing and **household** items.'

WORD FOCUS

A load of sth or **loads of sth** INF is a large number or amount of sth. SYNS **lots/masses/tons of sth.**

be after sth INF be trying to find sth.

cut-price sold at a reduced price.

clothing clothes in general. (A shirt is an *item of clothing*.)

pick sth up buy sth, especially cheaply or by chance.

bargain a thing bought for less than the usual price.

haggle (with sb) (over sth) argue with sb in order to reach an agreement, especially about the price of sth.

antique an old, often valuable object such as a piece of furniture or jewellery.

second-hand not new; owned by sb else before. OPP brand new.

bric-a-brac small objects of little value.

do a roaring trade INF sell a lot of sth very quickly.

gear sth towards sb/sth OFTEN PASSIVE prepare or organize sth so that it is suitable for a particular purpose.

rip-off INF a price that is too high for the value of sth. rip sb off v.

hustle and bustle busy, noisy activity of a lot of people in one place.

be into sth INF be interested in sth.

vintage typical of a period in the past, and of high quality: *vintage designs/cars*.

pricey INF expensive.

ethnic food, clothing, etc. from countries that are far away, which seem very different and unusual.

household (before a noun) used in the home.

13.3

Online shopping

ONLINE SHOPPING developed in the 1990s. It grew because transport costs went up, **telecom** costs came down, and internet access became **commonplace**. Webshops started **springing up** all over the internet, and they can now offer a larger range of **goods** than ordinary shops, at lower cost. The **drawback**, of course, is that you can't smell, touch, taste or try what you are buying.

In the past, **suppliers** mainly **targeted** women, but as online shopping has developed, the **target audience** has **widened▼** to include men as well.

It works like this. **Consumers** find a product they want on a website. They then add this product, or **multiple** products in some cases, to their '**basket**' (rather like a supermarket). They go through a '**checkout**' process (also like a supermarket) in which payment is collected and **delivery** instructions given. Most retailers then follow this up with email **confirmation** of the order.

WORD FOCUS
The suffix *–en* can be added to some adjectives, and a few nouns, to form verbs, e.g. **widen**, **deepen**, **weaken**, **strengthen**.

telecom INF (= telecommunications) communication over a distance by means of telephone, radio, TV, etc.

commonplace existing in many places, or done very often.

spring up appear or develop quickly.

goods PL N things that are produced to be sold: *leather/electrical goods*.

drawback SYN disadvantage.

supplier a person or company that provides sth and makes it available. supply sth v.

target sb OFTEN PASSIVE select sb as a possible buyer or user of your products or services. (A target audience is a particular group of people that a product is aimed at.)

widen become wider, or make sth wider.

consumer a person who buys goods or uses services. (A consumer society is one in which buying and selling is very important.)

multiple consisting of many people, things or parts: *multiple copies/injuries*.

basket this shows the item or items you have chosen to buy in an online shop.

checkout the part of the website where you enter your payment card details.

delivery the process of bringing goods to a place. deliver sth v.

confirmation a statement that sth will definitely happen at a particular time and in the way that it has been arranged. confirm sth v.

13.4 Clothes shopping

Clothes questionnaire

Write your answer in the box.

1 Do you ever buy **clothes** ▼ you like, even if they don't **suit** you?

2 Do you generally look for **baggy** clothes, **tight-fitting** clothes, or something **in between**?

3 When you buy something, do you normally consider whether you've got something that **goes with** it?

4 When you buy new clothes, do you usually look for a complete **outfit**?

5 Do you like buying clothes and **dressing up** for special occasions?

6 Does it matter to you whether you wear **designer labels**?

7 Have you ever bought any of these? A **waistcoat**, a **cardigan**, a **nightdress,** a pair of **pyjamas,** or a **bikini.**

WORD FOCUS

Clothes is a plural noun and **clothing** is an uncountable noun. We can use **clothing** to talk about clothes in general, one **item of clothing**, or clothes for a particular purpose, e.g. **waterproof clothing** (= clothes that keep you dry).

suit sb look good on sb.

baggy clothes that are baggy are very loose on your body. OPP tight or tight-fitting.

in between between one thing and another.

go with sth if one thing goes with another thing, the two things look good together.

outfit a set of clothes that you wear together.

dress up wear clothes that are more formal than you usually wear. OPP dress down.

designer (before a noun) made by a famous designer, e.g. Armani.

label the name of a fashion company; also used for the clothes it makes.

waistcoat

cardigan

nightdress

pyjamas

bikini

13.5 Getting things done

'I'm **getting** my watch **repaired** ▼, but I can't **pick** it **up** till next week.'

'My car is **coming up for** a **service**, and I've also got a small **dent** in the side, so I'll **get** that **fixed** then.'

'I'm going to the dentist for a **check-up** next week, and I think I need a **filling**.'

'I **had** my suit **cleaned** ▼ last week, but they didn't **make a very good job of** it. I won't use that **dry cleaner's** again.'

'I'm going to **have** my hair **cut** ▼ after work. I just want a **trim**.'

'I've **torn** my jacket, so I'll have to **get** it **mended**. I may **get** the **zip replaced** too; that shop does all sorts of **repairs**.'

tear   zip

WORD FOCUS

If you **have** or **get** something **cleaned/ repaired**, etc., somebody performs a service for you, which you pay for:
I **cut** my hair. = I cut it myself.
I **got/had** my hair **cut**. = somebody else cut my hair.

152

repair sth put sth that is broken, damaged or torn back into good condition. repair N.

pick sth up collect sth from a place.

come up for sth be reaching the time when sth must be done.

service an examination of a vehicle or machine to check that it works correctly and to make repairs. have sth serviced v.

dent a place where a surface has been damaged by being pushed or knocked inwards. dent sth v.

fix sth repair sth, especially an object or machine.

check-up a medical or dental examination to see if you are healthy or your teeth are in good condition.

filling a mixture that a dentist puts in your tooth to fill a hole.

make a good/bad job of sth do sth well/ badly, etc.

dry cleaner's a shop where clothes are cleaned using chemicals rather than water.

trim the act of cutting a small amount off sth, especially hair. trim sth v.

tear sth (PT tore PP torn) damage sth by pulling it apart or by cutting it on sth sharp. SYN rip sth. tear N. (see picture)

mend sth repair sth, especially clothes, or a small object such as a watch.

replace sth get sth new because the one you have or had is lost or damaged.

A typical house

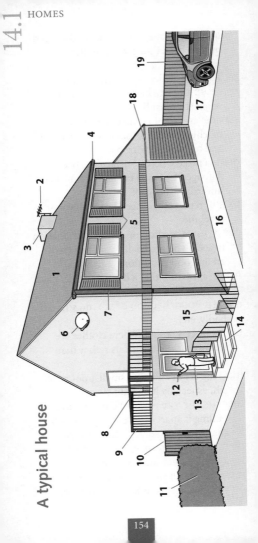

This is a **three-storey** house (= a house on three levels).

1 roof
2 aerial
3 chimney
4 gutter
5 shutters
6 satellite dish
7 drainpipe
8 balcony
9 railings ▶
10 gate ▶

11 hedge ▶
12 doorbell
13 front door
14 steps
15 basement
16 path
17 drive
18 garage
19 fence ▶

WORD FOCUS

A **fence, gate, hedge** and **railings** are types of **barrier** (= sth that stops people or cars from entering a place).
A **passage** is a long, narrow area with walls on either side; it can be indoors or outdoors. A **corridor** is a passage in a building or on a train and has doors leading to rooms or compartments from it.

155

Interiors

1 fireplace
2 mantelpiece
3 rug
4 vase
5 ornaments

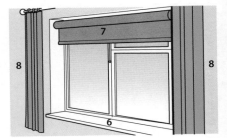

6 window sill
7 blind
8 curtains

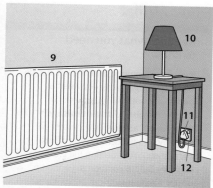

9 radiator
10 table lamp
11 plug
12 socket

13 mattress
14 pillow
15 sheet
16 duvet
17 blanket

14.3

Finding a flat

Renting: what you need to know

If you're planning to **rent** ▼ a flat, decide what type of **property** you need: a **bedsit**, a **studio flat** or something bigger? **Furnished** or **unfurnished**? What kind of **amenities** do you need **close by**? How much **can** you **afford** per month, not forgetting the **expense** of **utility bills** in addition to your **rental** ▼ **payments**?

You can find properties through a **letting agent** or on the internet. Once you have found a place, you will need to **sign a contract**; it is vital to read it carefully. As a new **tenant** ▼, you will need to pay your **landlord** ▼ a **deposit** which is usually the **equivalent** of a month's rent. **Insist on** a **receipt** for the deposit, and ask for an **inventory** of the contents and condition of the property.

WORD FOCUS

If you **rent** something, e.g. a house, you pay to use it for a long period of time. **rent** N, **rental** ADJ, N. If you **hire** something, you pay to use it for a short time, e.g. hire a bike for a day. You can **rent** or **hire** a car. If you rent a house, you become the **tenant**; the person you pay is the **landlord** or **landlady** (= the owner of the house).

property a building and the land around it.

bedsit a rented room that is used both for living and sleeping in.

studio flat a flat with one main room, a bathroom and a kitchen.

furnished (of a flat, house, etc.) with furniture. OPP **unfurnished**.

amenities things that make a place easy or comfortable to live in, e.g. shops, a bus service.

close by near.

afford sth if you can afford sth, you have enough money to pay for it.

expense an amount of money you spend to buy or do sth.

utility bill the amount you have to pay for services such as gas, electricity or water.

payment a sum of money paid.

letting agent sb who manages a property for the landlord.

contract an official written agreement: *sign a contract.*

deposit a sum of money that is paid by a tenant, but is later given back to the tenant if they do not damage the property.

equivalent equal in value.

insist on sth demand that sth happens.

receipt a piece of paper which shows that money has been paid for sth.

inventory a list of all the objects, furniture, etc. in a house or flat.

Renting and owning

'I **moved into** a flat two years ago and found a **flatmate** to help with the bills. I was paying €700 a month in rent, which was a lot for me, but recently the landlord **put** the rent **up** by 10% for all the tenants in the building. I decided not to **renew** the **tenancy** and **gave** him a month's **notice**.'

'We spent three years **saving up for** the **deposit** for a flat, and we finally found a lovely place through a local **estate agent**. We **made an offer** which the **vendor** accepted. We then had to **take out a mortgage** ▼, and use a **solicitor** to deal with the contract. But the trouble was that as soon as we moved in, the **interest rates rose** and the mortgage **went up**. It's now a **struggle** to pay every month, but we can't bear to **put** our lovely flat **on the market**.'

WORD FOCUS

When you **take out a mortgage** from a bank or similar organization, you borrow money to buy a house, flat, etc. You pay the money back every month over a number of years. You have to **pay interest** on this money (see page 161).

move into sth start to live in your new home. OPP **move out of sth**.

flatmate sb who shares a flat with one or more people; also **housemate**.

put sth up (by sth) increase the price of sth by a certain amount.

renew sth arrange for sth, e.g. a contract, to continue for a further period of time.

tenancy a period of time that you rent a flat/house for.

give sb notice give sb a warning in advance that sth is going to happen, often that you are going to leave somewhere.

save up for sth keep money instead of spending it so that you can use it for sth later.

deposit the first payment you make when you agree to buy sth expensive, e.g. a flat.

estate agent sb who sells houses and land for people.

make (sb) an offer say how much money you are willing to pay for sth.

vendor a person who is selling a house.

solicitor a lawyer who gives legal advice, prepares legal contracts, etc., especially for buying a house or land.

interest rate the percentage that a bank charges you on money that you borrow, or pays you on money that you keep in it.

rise (PT **rose** PP **risen**) increase. SYN **go up**.

struggle a hard fight to achieve sth.

put sth on the market try to sell sth.

14.5

Living in a flat

What are the **pros and cons** of flats?

✓ PROS:

- Flats are often more **secure** than houses, and less **prone to** burglary.
- They **are** often centrally **located**, and **handy** for shops, services, etc.
- Being on one **level** makes life easy, especially for **the disabled** or **elderly**.
- You don't usually have the **hassle** of the **upkeep** of a garden, as it is covered by the **service charge**.

✗ CONS:

- You have little control over the service charge, which can be **considerable**.
- You may have the **irritation** of noisy neighbours, especially if the flats don't have **soundproofed** walls.
- You may be prone to damage from **burst pipes** (see picture) above you.

- There may be **restrictions** in the **lease**, for example on **owning** pets.
- If you are in a **high-rise** building, you may have problems trying to leave your flat **in case of** fire.

pros and cons the advantages and disadvantages of sth.

secure safe from attack, harm or damage.

prone to sth likely to be affected by sth, often sth bad.

be located if sth is located in a particular place, it exists there or has been put there.

handy located in a convenient place.

level a floor of a building.

the disabled people who cannot use a part of their body properly.

the elderly a polite word for 'old people'.

hassle INF a situation that annoys you or causes you problems.

upkeep the work needed to keep sth in good condition. SYN maintenance.

service charge money that people in flats pay for the repair and management of the building.

considerable quite large. SYN significant.

irritation the feeling of being annoyed.

soundproofed designed to stop sound from entering or leaving.

restriction a rule or law that limits what you can do.

lease a legal agreement to rent or own a property for a particular period of time.

own sth if you own sth, it is yours; it belongs to you (= you are the owner).

high-rise very tall and with a lot of floors.

in case of sth if sth happens.

14.6

Home renovation

I've bought a nice property, but it's very **run-down** and needs some **renovation** ▼. Even basic **maintenance** has been poor. This is what has to be done:

- The house needs **redecorating** ▼ **throughout**.

- There are **blocked** sinks and **leaking** pipes: we'll have to **redo** some of the **plumbing**. Also, the **central heating** isn't **working properly** and we may have to **install** a new **system**.

- There are old **wires** everywhere, and some **faulty** sockets. We'll have to **re-wire** parts of the house.

- The windows are **in bad condition**. We can **restore** ▼ some, but one or two will need to be **replaced**.

- It'll need a new kitchen and bathroom.

But **once** it's **done up**, it will be great.

WORD FOCUS

If you **renovate** a building, you repair and paint it so that it is in good condition. **renovation** N. If you **redecorate**, you put new paint or paper on the walls. If you **restore** an object or part of a building, you repair it so that it looks as good as it did originally.

run-down in bad condition because nobody has spent money on repairs.

maintenance the work done to keep sth in good condition. SYN upkeep.

throughout in every part of a place.

blocked if a sink is blocked, sth is stopping water from passing through it.

leaking allowing liquid or gas to get through a small hole or crack. leak N, V.

redo sth do sth again or do sth differently.

plumbing the system of pipes, etc. that supply water to a building.

central heating a way of heating a building by sending hot air or water through pipes.

properly if sth is not working properly, it is not working correctly or well.

install sth put a piece of equipment somewhere and make it ready for use.

system a group of things or pieces of equipment that are connected together.

wire a long, thin piece of metal, covered in plastic, that is used to carry electricity: *electrical/telephone wires.*

faulty not working or made correctly.

re-wire sth put new electrical wires into a building or machine.

in good/bad condition in a good/bad physical state.

replace sth change sth that is old or damaged for sth that is new or better.

once as soon as; when.

do sth up repair and decorate sth.

Tools

1 screw

2 screwdriver you use a screwdriver to screw sth together or to a wall, etc. If you unscrew sth, you take the screw out.

3 nails

4 nut

5 bolt

6 hammer you use a hammer to hit nails into sth, or to break sth. Hammer is also a verb: *I hammered the nails into the fence.*

7 spanner you use a spanner for tightening or loosening nuts and bolts.

8 saw N. saw sth V.

9 (electric) drill you use a drill to drill holes in walls, wood, etc.

10 paintbrush

11 roller

12 ladder

Cleaning

ARE YOU a **houseproud** person who wants a **spotless** home, but hasn't time to do all those **household chores**? We at *MAID 4 YOU* can **carry out** all the cleaning **duties** you could possibly need!

- We will…**dust, polish, sweep, scrub, hoover,** and we will **wipe** all your kitchen cupboards and **surfaces.** We can even **tidy up** your **clutter!**

- We can… **deal with stains and spills!**

- We can… **do the laundry, the ironing, the washing-up** – you name it, we can do it.

- **No matter how** dirty your house, we will leave it looking **spick and span**.

Call us on 0777 888 888 today!

sweep

scrub

houseproud if you are houseproud, you always keep your house clean and tidy.

spotless perfectly clean. OPP filthy.

household relating to a home: *household chores, household bills*.

chore an ordinary job that has to be done regularly.

carry sth out do a particular piece of work.

duties PL N things that you have to do as part of your job or your responsibility.

dust sth remove very small pieces of dirt (=dust) from surfaces with a soft cloth.

polish sth make sth shiny by rubbing it.

hoover sth clean the floor with an electric machine (= hoover™ SYN vacuum cleaner).

wipe sth clean a surface with a soft cloth.

surface the flat area of a desk, table, counter, etc. which is used for working on.

tidy sth up make a place look better by putting things in the correct place.

clutter a lot of untidy things. SYN mess.

deal with sth take action to do sth.

stain a mark left accidentally on clothes or surfaces which is difficult to remove.

spill a quantity of liquid that has accidentally come out of its container. spill sth V.

do the laundry wash clothes, sheets, etc.

do the ironing iron clothes, etc.

do the washing-up wash dishes, etc.

no matter how/when/where, etc. = it doesn't matter how/when/where, etc.

spick and span very clean and tidy.

Bank statement

Account type: **Current**
Overdraft limit: £1,200

Account **Summary**	
Balance on 26 May 2012	£2,400.80
Total **Paid In**	£1,200.00
Total **Paid Out**	£1,828.34
Balance on 26 June	£1,772.46

Account Activity				
Date	Payment	Out	In	Balance
28/5	**DD**	48.50		£2,352.30

I generally use my current account to
pay most of my monthly **direct debits** –
mortgage, **personal pension**, bills, etc.
I also made a couple of **withdrawals** this
month, and I used my **debit card** several
times in shops. I usually have to make
one **deposit** each month to make sure I
stay **in credit** ▼.

WORD FOCUS

If money is **credited to** your account,
it is paid into your account. If money is
debited from your account, it is taken
out. If your account is **in credit**, it has
money in it. If you have a **minus** (-)
figure in your account, you are **in the
red/overdrawn**.

bank statement a printed or online record of the money paid into and out of your account within a particular period.

current account a type of account where you can take out money at any time.

overdraft an arrangement with a bank that allows you to spend more money than is in your account.

summary a short account of sth that gives only the most important information.

(bank) balance the amount of money that you have in your bank account.

pay sth in put money into a bank account.

pay sth out pay a sum of money for sth.

DD ABBREV **direct debit** an instruction to your bank to allow sb else to take money from your account on a particular date.

mortgage a legal agreement in which you borrow money in order to buy a flat or house; you pay it back every month over a period of time.

(personal) pension a system of paying money regularly into a fund, which then provides you with money when you stop working and retire.

withdrawal the act of taking money out of your bank account. **withdraw sth** v.

debit card a plastic card given by a bank that you use to pay for things.

deposit a sum of money that is paid into a bank account. **deposit sth** v.

Salaries

In 2010, a British MP (Member of Parliament) was paid a basic **salary** ▼ of just over £63,000, but many MPs **claimed** twice that amount a year **on expenses**, which included staff pay, stationery and travel costs. MPs who did not live in London **were** also **entitled to** an **allowance** of **up to** £24,000 a year towards the cost of a second home. This may seem like a good **living**, but it's still a **pittance** compared with people working in the **financial sector**, many of whom receive a **massive** annual **bonus on top of** their salaries. Senior city bankers, for example, can **boost** their **earnings** by £1m just from their annual bonus, and even more junior members of staff can **make** a lot of money.

WORD FOCUS

A **salary** is money that professional employees or office staff **earn** for doing a job. It is usually paid every month and expressed as an **annual** (= yearly) figure. **Wages** are usually paid every day/week or month to people doing manual jobs. The total amount a person earns is their **income. Income tax** is what you must pay to the government based on what you earn.

claim sth ask for money from a company or the government because you have a right to it. claim N.

expenses PL N money you spend while you are working which your employer will pay back to you later (claim sth on expenses).

be entitled to sth be given the right to have or do sth.

allowance an amount of money that you are allowed for a particular purpose: *a clothing/travel/living allowance* as part of your job.

up to sth as far as a particular number, level, etc., but not more.

living money that you earn to live on. (What do you do for a living? = What's your job?)

pittance an amount of money that is so small it seems unfair.

sector a part of an area of activity, especially of a country's economy: *the financial sector*. (The public sector is that part of a country's economy owned by the government. OPP the private sector.)

massive very large in amount or degree. SYNS huge, enormous.

bonus extra money that you are paid in addition to your salary, often once a year.

on top (of sth) in addition (to sth).

boost sth help sth to increase or improve.

earnings the amount of money you earn.

make sth earn sth.

Getting into debt

I managed to **put aside** some money before I went to university, and I also got a **grant** because my parents don't earn a great deal. However, after I'd paid my **tuition fees** and bought a lot of books, I still had to **take out** a **loan** to **cover the cost of** my living **expenses**. By the end of my first year I already **owed** the student loan company over £4,000.

In my second year, my parents **subsidized** me where they could, and I **dipped into** my **savings** a bit more as well, but my **debts** ▼ still **mounted up**. By the time I finished my degree, I owed over £15,000 at 5% **interest**. It will take me years to **pay that off**.

WORD FOCUS

A **debt** [/det/] is an amount of money that you **owe sb** (see page 175). You can **get into debt** or **be in debt**, and in this situation you will try to **settle your debts** (= pay back all of it).

put sth aside save sth or keep it available to use.

grant a sum of money that is given by the government or other organization to be used for a particular purpose: *a student/research grant*.

tuition fees money that a student has to pay for the teaching they receive.

take sth out apply for or pay for an official document or service: *take out insurance/a loan*.

loan an amount of money that sb borrows, especially from a bank.

cover the cost of sth provide enough money for sth.

expenses an amount of money you spend in order to do sth: *living/travel expenses*.

owe (sb) sth have to pay sb for sth you have already received, or return money that you have borrowed.

subsidize sb/sth give money to a person or an organization to help them pay for sth. **subsidy** N.

dip into sth take some money from an amount that you have saved.

savings PL N money that you have saved.

mount up increase gradually in size.

interest extra money that you pay back when you borrow money, or extra money you receive when you invest money.

pay sth off finish paying the money you owe for sth.

15.4

Shopping

I hate clothes shopping, but about twice a year I **force myself to** go out and buy a few things. I tend to think most clothes are a **rip-off**, so I generally wait for **the sales** when I'm more likely to find some good **reductions** and **bargains**. I never buy anything unless it has at least 20% **off**, and even then I'm prepared to **haggle** in the shop to get a bit more off. It's not always a successful policy, though. My last **buy** ▼ was a coat which I didn't like when I got home, so I had to take it back to the shop to try and get a **refund**.

My sister thinks I'm just **mean**, but I'd never **make ends meet** if I was like her. She's a real **spendthrift**, and seems to go on a **shopping spree** about twice a month. And she's quite prepared to **pay a fortune** for jeans just because they have a designer label on the back. I think she's mad.

WORD FOCUS

Buy can also be a noun (sth that you buy), e.g. *That winter coat was one of my best buys.* SYN **purchase** N,V. FML. A **buyer** is someone who buys sth expensive, e.g. *I haven't found a buyer for my flat.*

force sb/yourself to do sth make sb do sth that they do not want to do.

rip-off INF sth that is more expensive than it should be. (If you **rip sb off**, you cheat them by charging them too much for sth.)

the sales a period of time when shops sell goods at a lower price than normal.

reduction an amount of money by which sth is made cheaper. **reduce sth** v.

bargain sth bought for a good price, and often lower than the usual price.

off used for saying that a price has been reduced by a particular amount.

haggle (with sb) argue with sb in order to reach an agreement, especially over the price of sth. **haggling** N.

refund a sum of money that is returned to you, especially when you have decided you no longer want sth.

mean not willing to spend money. SYNS **stingy, tight** INF.

make ends meet have just enough money to buy the things that you need.

spendthrift DISAPPROVING sb who is very careless about money and spends more than they need to.

spree a period of time spent in an uncontrolled way on an activity you enjoy: *a shopping/spending spree.*

fortune a large amount of money. (You can **pay a fortune** for sth, and sth can **cost a fortune**.)

Raising money for charity

Fundraising for charity

Guy North and Ben Greenall plan to walk almost 600 miles from Portsmouth to Glasgow as part of an **appeal in aid of** the charity 'Understanding diabetes'. They have already received a large number of **donations** from family and friends, and have **raised** over £5,000. At this **rate** ▼, they should reach their **target** of £12,000 **in no time**.

Guy and Ben have **supported** the charity for several years, but say they are **desperately in need of** more money and more **volunteers**. 'It's a wonderful **cause**', said Ben, who now hopes that his firm will **sponsor** him to walk part of the Andes next year. ●

WORD FOCUS

A **rate** can be the speed at which sth happens (as above), but it can also be a fixed amount of money paid for something, e.g. the **exchange rate** ($1= €1.2), or how often something happens, e.g. the **birth rate**.

fundraising the activity of collecting money for a charity. (A **fund** is an amount of money that has been saved or made available for a particular purpose.)

charity an organization which helps people who are poor, sick, etc.

appeal an urgent request for people to give you sth that you need such as help, money or information. **appeal (to sb) (for sth)** v.

in aid of sth/sb in order to help sth/sb.

donation a sum of money that is given to a person or charity. **donate sth** v.

raise money collect money for a particular reason.

target a result that you try to achieve/reach.

in no time very quickly or very soon. SYN **in next to no time**.

support sb/sth give sb/sth help and often money. **support** N.

desperately extremely; very much.

in need of sth in a situation when sth is necessary. (Also **a need for sth**, e.g. *There's an urgent need for more money.*)

volunteer sb who offers to help sb, or chooses to do a job, without being paid. **volunteer for sth** v.

cause an aim, idea or organization that you support or work for.

sponsor sb give sb money for a charity if they succeed in completing a particular activity. **sponsorship** N. A person who gives this money is a **sponsor**.

Road signs

1

2

3

4

5

GIVE WAY

6

7

8

9

1   **50** mph speed limit = you must not travel faster than 50 miles per hour (about 80 kph/kilometres per hour).

2   **no through road** (also called a **dead end**) a road that is closed at one end to vehicles (= cars, buses, lorries, etc.).

3   **crossroads** where two roads cross each other.

4   The road **bends** to the right. You may also see a sign where the road **bends** to the left. **bend** N: *a bend in the road.*

5   **no overtaking** = you must not pass another vehicle that is travelling in the same direction. **overtake** sb V.

6   **give way to oncoming vehicles** cars, buses, etc. coming in the opposite direction are allowed to enter this part of the road before you do; they have **priority**, and you must **give way** to them.

7   **pedestrian crossing** (also called a **zebra crossing**) a part of the road where vehicles must stop and allow **pedestrians** (= people on foot) to cross.

8   **roundabout** ▼ in the UK vehicles must give way to traffic coming from the right at a **roundabout**.

9   **slippery road** a road which is difficult to move on, usually because it is wet or icy.

WORD FOCUS

A **crossroads** and a **roundabout** are two types of road **junction** (= the place where two or more roads meet).

Cars

The new A7, **manual** or **automatic**, offers **outstanding performance**, and now comes with more **fuel**-efficient engines.

1 rear-view mirror

2 windscreen

3 wing mirror

4 **dashboard** All the instruments are shown on the dashboard.

5 satnav ABBREV satellite navigation (also called GPS = Global Positioning System).

6 **steering wheel** used to steer the car.

7 **horn** the object in a car that makes a loud, warning noise when you press it.

8 **gear lever** used to change gear, e.g. from first to second, or second to third.

9 **clutch** You need to put your foot on the clutch in order to change gear.

10 **brake** used to make the car slow down or stop. put on the brakes.

11 **accelerator** used to make the car go faster. accelerate v; acceleration N.

12 **seat belt** You fasten your seat belt when you get in the car.

automatic in an automatic car, the gears change by themselves without any action by the driver. OPP manual.

outstanding extremely good. SYN superb.

performance (of a car or machine) the capacity to operate fast and efficiently.

fuel a material or substance such as petrol, oil, or gas, that produces heat or power.

16.3

Public transport

What are your views on public transport?

'We need **reliable** and **affordable** public transport in order to reduce the number of cars and **ease congestion**.'

'I hate public transport in the **rush hour**. The Underground ▼ is **packed** and buses take **forever**.'

'You are **restricted** with public transport. Cars are more **convenient**, and I enjoy the **freedom of movement**.'

'Cars **pollute** the atmosphere, and our roads weren't designed for all the traffic we have now. Better public transport would lower the **carbon footprint**.'

'**Motorists** will never **give up** their cars while public transport is so expensive. It needs to be more heavily **subsidized**.'

'Buses **run** every ten minutes, but you do get **hold-ups** during the rush hour, and I hate having to **queue**.'

WORD FOCUS

The underground railway system in London is called **the Underground** (also called **the Tube**); in New York it is called **the subway**. In British English, a **subway** is a passage that goes under the ground for people to walk through.

reliable a reliable system is one that works well. OPP unreliable.

affordable cheap enough for ordinary people to use or buy. afford sth v.

ease sth make a problem, bad situation or a pain less severe.

congestion the state of being crowded and full of traffic. congested ADJ.

rush hour the time when a lot of people are travelling to or from work.

packed very crowded.

forever an extremely long time.

restrict sb stop sb from moving or acting freely. restriction N.

convenient useful, easy or practical. OPP inconvenient. convenience N.

freedom of movement the state of being able to move around freely with no restrictions.

pollute sth make air, rivers, etc. dirty and harmful. pollution N.

carbon footprint a measure of the amount of carbon dioxide produced by sb or sth.

motorist sb who drives a car.

give sth up stop doing or using sth.

subsidize sth if a government subsidizes sth, it pays some of its cost so that is is cheaper for people. subsidy N.

run travel at a particular time.

hold-up INF a delay.

queue wait for sth in a line of people.

16.4

A road accident

A: There was a **nasty** accident here yesterday.

B: Really? What happened?

A: Well, I didn't see it myself, but **apparently** a car **shot out of** Brook Lane and **collided with** ▼ a car coming down the main road.

B: Oh, **my goodness**.

A: Yeah. And cars all around were **swerving** and **skidding** to **get out of the way**. One **crashed into** ▼ the newsagent's over there–that's why the window is **boarded up**.

B: Oh I see. Anyone injured?

A: **Thankfully** no, but at least one of the cars was a **write-off**. And when I came down about twenty minutes later, the road was still **blocked**, and there was a **massive tailback**.

WORD FOCUS

If two vehicles **crash,** or **crash into** each other, they hit each other very hard and cause a lot of damage. You can also use the verbs **collide (with sth),** which is more formal, or **smash into sth**, which is more informal.
If you **clip sth**, you just hit the edge or side of sth, usually without causing much damage.

nasty very bad or unpleasant (often used about an accident, injury, etc.).

apparently according to what you have heard or read.

shoot out of sth move suddenly and quickly out of a place.

my goodness INF used to express surprise.

swerve (of a vehicle) change direction suddenly, usually to avoid hitting sth/sb.

skid (usually of a vehicle) move sideways in an uncontrolled way, usually after the driver has braked suddenly. skid N.

get out of the way move away from or avoid the route that others are taking. (Also used as a command, e.g. *I'm coming, so get out of the/my way.*)

board sth up cover a door, window, etc. with wooden boards.

thankfully used to show that you are pleased that sth good has happened, or that sth bad has not happened. SYNS fortunately, luckily.

write-off a vehicle that has been too badly damaged to be repaired. write sth off v.

block sth stop people, traffic, etc. from moving along or through sth. SYN obstruct sth.

massive very large. SYNS huge, enormous.

tailback a long line of traffic that is moving slowly or not at all because of a problem on the road.

Air travel

Flying High

By 1960, **commercial aviation** was **flourishing** and a number of companies were offering a range of **scheduled flights**. Then, in the 1970s, *South West Airlines* in the US started operating the first **charter flights** and was hugely successful.

Since then, **airlines** ▼ have introduced **innovations** in both **domestic** and **international** air travel in order to offer a more personalized experience–for instance, to **guarantee** an **aisle seat**, or provide more **overhead locker** space. However, in a recent **survey**, most customer complaints were still to do with **inadequate legroom**, flight delays, missing **connecting flights**, and issues with airport **security**.

WORD FOCUS

Many words are formed using **air**:
aircraft any plane, **helicopter** or other vehicle that flies.
airline a company that owns aircraft.
air traffic control the activity of organizing the movement of planes.
airborne in the air.
aircrew the pilot and other people who work on a plane when it is flying.

commercial connected with the buying and selling of a product.

aviation the design and flying of aircraft.

flourish develop quickly and be successful. SYN thrive.

scheduled flight a flight that leaves at a regular time every day or week.

charter flight a flight in which the seats are sold at a lower cost than a scheduled flight, but without the same services.

innovation the introduction of new things, ideas or ways of doing sth. innovate v.

domestic of or inside a particular country. SYN national. OPP international.

guarantee sth if you guarantee sth, you promise to do sth or that sth will happen.

aisle seat a seat next to the aisle (= the passage between the seats).

overhead locker the small cupboard above your seat where you store things such as hand luggage.

survey a set of questions that you ask a group of people in order to get their views.

inadequate not good enough for a particular purpose or need. OPP adequate.

legroom space for your legs.

connecting flight a flight that you take to continue your journey after you get off a plane.

security activities that make people or buildings safe from attack, danger, etc.

Sea travel

1

2

3

4

5

6

7

1 A passenger ship is used to carry passengers (= move them from one place to another). Large passenger ships which travel long distances are called liners.

2 A ferry is used to take people and/or vehicles across a river or a narrow part of a sea. A ferry may be a boat or quite a large ship.

3 A freighter or cargo ship is used to carry goods from one place to another; the goods are the freight or cargo. A ship that is used to carry oil or petrol is called an oil tanker.

4 A yacht is a boat that you sail.

5 A fishing boat is used to catch fish. A fishing boat that uses large nets to catch fish is called a trawler.

6 A rowing boat usually requires at least one person with two oars (see picture) to row the boat.

7 A canoe usually requires at least one person with a paddle (see picture) to paddle the canoe.

WORD FOCUS

When you get on a ship, you **board** it or **embark** FML; when you get off, you **go ashore** or **disembark** FML. While you are on the ship you are **on board**. A long journey by ship is called a **voyage**, and a holiday by ship in which you stop at different places is called a **cruise**.

17.1

Types of holiday

holiday–online.com

Whether you're looking for a romantic **break**, a **tropical** beach **resort** or an **all-inclusive** holiday, we can **cater for** all your needs with first-class **hospitality** and **exceptional** service.

Experience a little bit of **paradise** on one of our **package tours** to a wide range of **destinations**! Tours include accommodation, flights and **transfers**.

Why not try a **spa** break? It's a great way to escape from the stress of daily life. **Chill out** in one of our **luxurious** spa resorts for a **unique** and highly **memorable** experience.

Or **soak up** the sun on one of our relaxing **cruises** ▼. Sail round the Mediterranean and **stop off** for **a bit of sightseeing** ▼ along the way.

WORD FOCUS

You can **go on a cruise** (= go on a holiday by ship where you stop at different places), or **cruise down** the Nile/**around** the Bahamas. You can **go sightseeing/see the sights** (=visit interesting places as a tourist), or **do a bit of/a lot of sightseeing**.

break a short holiday.

tropical in or from the hottest parts of the world.

resort a place where a lot of people go on holiday: *ski/beach resort*.

all-inclusive including everything, i.e. the cost of accommodation, food, etc.

cater for sb/sth provide things that a person or a situation needs.

hospitality friendly to guests and making them feel welcome.

exceptional extremely good.

experience sth if you experience a situation, you are in that situation.

paradise a perfect place.

package tour a holiday with travel and hotel organized by a company for a fixed price.

destination a place where sb is going.

transfer the act of changing to a different place or vehicle on a journey.

spa a place with a pool where you go to relax and improve your health.

chill out INF spend time relaxing.

luxurious very expensive and comfortable. luxury N.

unique different from anything else.

memorable so special or good that you will remember it.

soak sth up INF spend time experiencing sth enjoyable: *soak up the sun/the atmosphere*.

stop off make a short visit somewhere during a longer trip.

Why travel?

'I'm **off to** Bern **on business**, then I'm going to **attend** a conference in Zug.'

'We're just going to **meet up with** family who are living **overseas**.'

'I'm going to Japan. I just want the **chance** ▼ to learn the language.'

'I'm going to India–I'm curious about **faraway** places, and I want to **get to know** people from other cultures and understand their **way of life**. It's a way of **broadening my horizons**, really.'

'We're both **in a rut** and need a change. We just want to **get away from it all** and **unwind**, so we're off to Zanzibar.'

'Actually, I'm **emigrating** to Australia!'

'It's my **gap year**, and I'm going to do some **voluntary work** in a **developing country** before I go to university.'

'Dad and I are going on a **pilgrimage**.'

WORD FOCUS

A **chance** or an **opportunity** is a time or a situation when it is possible to do something that you want to do. **Opportunity** is a little more formal. You can **take/seize/miss/turn down a chance/an opportunity**.

be off (to a place) leave a place to go to another place.

on business if you are away on business, you are away for work, not for pleasure.

attend sth RATHER FML go to an event, e.g. a conference, a meeting.

meet up with sb meet sb, especially by arrangement.

overseas in a country separated from your country by sea.

faraway a long distance away.

get to know sb/sth spend time with sb/ sth so that you learn more about them.

way of life the typical way in which a person or group lives.

broaden your horizons increase your experience and knowledge of life.

in a rut having a boring way of life that is difficult to change.

get away from it all go somewhere different to have a rest or a holiday.

unwind INF begin to relax after working hard.

emigrate leave your country in order to live in another country.

gap year a year, usually between school and university, when you can work or travel.

voluntary work work you do for no pay, usually to help sb.

developing country a country that is poor and is trying to improve its economy.

pilgrimage a journey that a religious person makes to a holy place.

Guide books

Come to Devon and Cornwall!

- **Wander** around the **magnificent ▼ nature reserve** and **bird sanctuary**
- See the **glorious ▼** gardens at Lyme Bay
- Visit Paignton Zoo: home to many **endangered species**
- See Tintagel, **legendary** home of King Arthur and part of our national **heritage**
- Visit Castle Drogo, a copy of a **medieval fortress**, with its **grand ▼** reception rooms
- Powderham Castle, set in **spectacular ▼** scenery with **breathtaking** views, makes an **enchanting** day out for the family
- **Marvel at** the **exquisite** jewels and **exotic** shells amongst the **treasures** at Lee Court
- Bradworthy Transport Museum **houses** over 80 historic vehicles, including tractors **dating back to** 1914.

WORD FOCUS

Magnificent countryside or scenery is extremely beautiful and impressive. SYN **spectacular**.

Glorious is very similar in meaning, but also describes sth which is bright and colourful.

A **grand** building is impressive and large or important.

wander walk slowly around a place, often without any particular purpose or direction.

nature reserve an area of natural land where plants and animals are protected.

sanctuary a special area where animals live in a protected natural environment: *wildlife/bird sanctuary*.

endangered species a type of animal or plant that may soon become extinct (= disappear from the world).

legendary from a very old story that may or may not be true.

heritage the art, buildings, beliefs, etc. that a society considers important to its history and culture.

medieval relating to the period in European history from 1000 to 1500.

fortress a large strong building used for defending an important place.

breathtaking very exciting and impressive.

enchanting very attractive and pleasing.

marvel at sth be impressed or surprised by sth.

exquisite very beautiful and delicate.

exotic unusual and interesting, and usually coming from a distant country.

treasure a piece of art or historical object that is very valuable.

house sth provide a place for sth.

date back to sth have existed since a particular time in the past.

Accommodation

'We stayed at a **B and B** ▼ **just off** the seafront called 'Abbey Lodge' which was **set** in its own **grounds** and was very **convenient for** the shops and restaurants. It's owned by a charming Scottish couple who were extremely **hospitable**. We had a **spacious, en-suite** room with the added **bonus** that it **overlooked** the sea. **Highly recommended**.'

'This year we decided to try a **self-catering cottage** ▼ which was on a farm. It was a bit **isolated**, but the cottage had a **cosy** feel downstairs, and the kitchen was **well equipped**. The bedrooms, though, were rather **cramped** and **dingy**. We were there **out of season**, so the **rates** were very reasonable.'

WORD FOCUS

A **B and B** (= bed and breakfast) is a private house where you sleep and have breakfast. A **guest house** is a small hotel or private house with guest rooms. A **hostel** provides cheap rooms for travellers or students.
Some holidaymakers rent a **cottage** (= a small house usually in the country), or a **villa** (= a holiday home, especially in Southern Europe).

just off near a particular road but not directly on it.

set if sth is set somewhere, it is in that place or position.

grounds PL N the land or garden around a large building.

convenient (for sth) near a place or easy to get to. SYN handy (for sth).

hospitable generous and friendly to guests. SYN welcoming.

spacious large and having space to move around in. OPP cramped.

en-suite an en-suite bedroom has a bathroom joined to it.

bonus another pleasant thing in addition to sth you were expecting: *added bonus*.

overlook sth have a view of sth from above.

highly recommended = considered to be very good.

self-catering (of accommodation) where you cook your own meals.

isolated far away from other places. SYN remote.

cosy warm, comfortable and safe, and often quite small.

well equipped with all the things you need.

dingy dark, unpleasant and dirty.

out of season at the time of year when most people do not go to a place. OPP in peak season.

rate a fixed amount of money that sth costs or sb is paid.

17.5

Travel complaints

'We **were due to** leave at 3.00, but the flight **was delayed** ▼ for over four hours. I knew that we **were entitled to** free **refreshments**, but we were given none.'

'The 6.00 train **was cancelled**, so I got the 6.30, but that meant I missed my **connection** in Paris.'

'My bags **went missing** after a flight to Bali. I waited ages for **compensation**.'

'The flight was **overbooked**, so we couldn't get on. They said they'd put us **on standby**, but we decided to go by train instead. We **demanded** a **refund**, but they refused to **reimburse** us.'

'The train started to **fill up** and after a few **stops** it was really **overcrowded**. I found a seat, but I had to **give it up** to an elderly lady.'

WORD FOCUS

If your plane is **delayed** or **held up**, it will leave late (= not **on time**). These verbs are often used in the passive. You can also say *We had a delay/a hold-up* N.
If your trip is **postponed** or **put off**, someone will arrange for it to happen at a later time or date.

200

be due to do sth expect or be expected
   to do sth.

be entitled to sth/to do sth have a right
   to sth or to do sth.

refreshments sth light to eat or drink.

cancel sth If your flight is cancelled, sb
   has decided that it will not leave at
   all, and you have to take a later flight.
   cancellation N.

connection a train, flight, etc. that you
   take to continue your journey after you
   get off another train, flight, etc.

go missing if sth goes missing, it is lost or
   not in its usual place.

compensation money you receive for bad
   service, damage or injury.

overbooked if a flight is overbooked, the
   airline has sold more tickets than there
   are seats.

on standby ready to get on a plane if
   there is a seat left when it is about to
   take off.

demand sth ask for sth forcefully.

refund an amount of money paid back
   to you, especially if you are not happy
   about goods or services that you have
   bought.

reimburse sb FML pay back money to sb
   who has spent or lost it because of you.

fill up become full of people.

stop the place where a train or bus stops
   to let passengers get on or off.

overcrowded filled with too many people.

give sth up give sth to sb who needs it.

18.1

Discussing novels

Here are some general questions you can use for discussing novels:

What is the **significance** of the **title** of the **novel**?

Did the **plot grab your attention**, or did it take you a while to **get into it**?

Did you like the way the book is **structured**? For example, the use of **flashbacks** ▼.

Which **themes** are well **explored**?

What are the main **character**'s major **traits**, and what **motivates** their actions?

Which characters do you **identify with**?

Does the novel **depict** life at a particular time? If so, does it **shed** much **light on** that time?

Which **passages** did you find **insightful** or **profound**?

If there is **dialogue** in the novel, does it sound **authentic**?

Is the **ending** satisfying?

WORD FOCUS

Some books contain **flashbacks** (= scenes set in an earlier time than the main story). Most stories are told **chronologically** (= in the order in which events happened).

significance the meaning of sth.

title the name of a book, painting, etc.

novel a book that tells a story about imaginary people and events. (The writer is called a novelist.)

plot the series of events that form the story of a play, book, film, etc.

grab your attention if sth grabs your attention, it makes you interested in it.

get into sth INF start enjoying sth.

structure sth plan or organize sth.

theme the main subject of a book, film, etc.

explore sth examine or discuss sth carefully.

character a person in a novel, play, etc.

trait a particular quality in sb's character.

motivate sb make sb behave in a particular way.

identify with sb feel that you understand sb and share their feelings.

depict sth describe sth in words or pictures.

shed light on sth provide information that helps you understand sth.

passage a short section from a text, piece of music, etc.

insightful showing a good understanding of sb/sth. insight N.

profound showing serious thought.

dialogue the words that characters speak in a book, play, etc.

authentic true and accurate.

ending the way that a book, film, etc. ends.

18.2

A famous artist

VINCENT VAN GOGH'S **works** are famous for their **striking** colour, **coarse brushstrokes**, and simple but unforgettable **composition**. Although most famous for his many **oil paintings**, he also did hundreds of **sketches** which he included in letters to friends and family. Among his **masterpieces** are *Starry Night* (a **landscape**), *Sunflowers* (a **still life**), and *The Potato Eaters* (a **scene** consisting of five **figures** around a table). His **self-portraits** are also widely admired; it is believed that he painted himself as he could not afford to pay **models** to **pose** for **portraits**.

Van Gogh was **influenced** by the French Impressionists (Monet, Renoir, etc.) but he **is** most **associated with** Gauguin, with whom he worked closely. Together they made **canvases** of a coarse material. This caused them to paint thickly using heavy brushstrokes, which produced their **distinctive** style.

work a painting, book, piece of music, etc.

striking interesting and unusual.

coarse rough, irregular. OPP smooth.

brushstroke a mark of paint left on a surface
by the movement of a paint brush.

composition the arrangement of people
or objects in a painting or photograph.

oil painting a picture painted with
oil paints.

sketch a simple picture that is drawn
quickly.

masterpiece a work of art, e.g. a painting, a
book, that is the best example of sb's work.

landscape a painting of an area of land.

still life a painting of objects, e.g. fruit, pots.

scene a painting or drawing of a place and
the things/people in it.

figure a picture of a person.

self-portrait a picture of you that you
draw or paint yourself. (A portrait is a
picture of sb else.)

model sb whose job is to be painted,
drawn, etc. by an artist or photographer.

pose sit or stand in a particular position
in order to be drawn, painted, etc.

influence sb affect the way sb behaves
or acts, especially by giving them an
example to follow.

be associated with sth/sb be connected
with sb/sth in some way.

canvas a strong, woven material on which
artists paint using oil paints.

distinctive having a special quality that is
different and easy to recognize.

18.3 Acting in films

I've acted in lots of films, but I've never **made it big**. I started out doing small **parts**, and once I had a **supporting role** in a **low-budget** movie, but I've never played **the lead**.

My work's very varied. I've done **voice-overs** for TV adverts and films, which is great fun. I've also done a bit of **dubbing into** English on Japanese films, though personally I'd rather watch a foreign film with **subtitles**.

The last **feature film** I did was the **sequel** to 'Time Lords', which was **shot** in the Himalayas. The **cast** and **crew** found the conditions hard, but the **stuntmen** didn't seem to notice the cold. People think being in a film must be exciting, but when you're **on location**, you spend hours just sitting around.

I always go and see films I've been in when they **come out**, and occasionally I'm invited to the **premiere**. Some actors can't watch themselves, but I think it's nice to see your name in the **credits**.

make it big INF be very successful.

part the character played by an actor. *a good/big/small part*. SYN role.

supporting role used of a part in a film or play that is important but not the main role.

low-budget made with very little money.

the lead the main part in a film.

voice-over words spoken by an actor who is not seen on the screen.

dubbing the process of replacing the original speech in a film with words in another language. **dub sth (into sth)** v.

subtitles words that translate what is said in a film into another language, appearing at the bottom of the screen.

feature film a full-length film with a story.

sequel a film, book, etc. that continues the story of an earlier one.

shoot sth take photos or make a film of sth.

cast the group of actors in a film, play, etc.

crew a group of people with special skills working together: *film/ambulance crew*.

stuntman/woman sb who acts dangerous scenes in a film in place of an actor.

on location at a place where a film is being made away from a studio.

come out (of a film, book, etc.) become available to see or buy.

premiere the first performance of a play or film.

credits the list of people involved in the film shown at the end.

18.4

The theatre

*What did you think of the **play** ▼?*

'For me, it's a **triumph**. I love the **script** – it's brilliant. It starts slowly, but the **tension builds** to an astonishing **climax** in the final **scene** ▼.'

'The **role** of Dr Ellis is **played by** Jonny Farmer, who's **on stage** throughout the play. At first, I found him **unconvincing**, and he forgot his **lines** in a couple of places. But, by the end he **conveyed** the sense of fear well. Perhaps he just needed more time to **rehearse**.'

'The story's very **moving**, and **judging by** the **applause**, the **audience** really liked it. It **captures** the atmosphere of pre-war Europe well, and the **costumes** are great.'

'At the end of a boring first **act** ▼, I considered leaving at the **interval**, but there were some **touching** scenes in Act 2, and Act 3 was **gripping**.'

WORD FOCUS

A **play** (= a piece of work performed in a theatre) is usually divided into two or three **acts** (= sections of a play). Each act may have several **scenes** (= a part of an act in which events happen in one place).

triumph a great success.

script the words written for a play, film, etc.

tension a feeling of fear or excitement.

build gradually become stronger.

climax the most exciting part towards the end of a play, film, etc.

role an actor's part: *play a role/part*.

on stage on the raised area where actors perform.

unconvincing not seeming true or real.

lines the words spoken by an actor.

convey sth communicate an idea or feeling.

rehearse (sth) spend time practising a play, concert, etc. before a performance. rehearsal N.

moving causing deep feelings of sadness or sympathy. SYN touching.

judging by sth used for giving the reason why you think sth is true.

applause the sound of many people hitting their hands together to show enjoyment. applaud v. SYN clap.

audience a group of people who have come to a place to see a performance.

capture sth express what sb/sth is like in a way that people recognize.

costume a set of clothes that an actor wears in a play.

interval a short break between parts of a play, concert, etc.

gripping very interesting and exciting.

Classical music quiz

cello

trumpet

1 What kind of **instrument** is a **cello**? **Strings, percussion** or **brass**?

2 In which section of an **orchestra** would you find a **trumpet**?

3 Who **composed** *Rigoletto*?

4 Is Spanish singer Placido Domingo a **tenor** or a **bass**?

5 Is American singer Renée Fleming a **soprano** or an **alto**?

6 Which **composer**, born in 1770, wrote nine **symphonies**?

7 Was Herbert von Karajan a **conductor** or a composer?

8 Is **choral** music written for singers or for instruments alone?

9 Is a **pianist** an instrument or a **musician**?

10 Does an **overture** come at the beginning or the end of an opera?

11 How many **pieces of music** did Mozart write – 200, 400, or 600?

12 How many instruments are played in a **quartet**?

(Answers on page 377)

instrument a device for producing music, e.g. a guitar or piano.

strings PL N a group of instruments in an orchestra that have strings, e.g. violins.

percussion a group of instruments you play by hitting them, e.g. drums.

brass a group of instruments made of metal that you play by blowing them, e.g. horns.

orchestra a large group of musicians who play different instruments together.

compose sth write a piece of music. Sb who writes classical music is a composer.

tenor a man's singing voice at the highest of the adult male range.

bass the lowest man's singing voice.

soprano the highest singing voice for a woman, boy or girl.

alto the lowest woman's singing voice.

symphony a long piece of classical music performed by an orchestra.

conductor sb who directs an orchestra or group of musicians. conduct sth/sb v.

choral connected with, or sung by a group of singers. (The group is called a choir.)

pianist a person who plays the piano.

musician a person who plays an instrument or writes music, especially as a job.

overture a piece of music written as the introduction to an opera or ballet.

piece of music a single item of music that sb has created.

quartet a group of four musicians or singers.

18.6 Rock music

Kings of Leon is an American rock band from Tennessee. Caleb Followill plays **rhythm guitar** and is **lead vocalist**, his brother Nathan plays drums and provides **backing vocals**, with two further group members, brother Jared and cousin Matthew on **bass guitar**, **lead guitar** and backing vocals.

Kings of Leon have had nine **singles** ▼ in **the** UK **charts**, two BRIT **awards**, with their third **album** ▼, *Because of the Times*, getting to **number one**.

Their latest album, *Come around Sundown*, was **recorded** in New York and **released** in the UK in October 2010. Here's what **critic** Sonny Lee says:

'It's **polished** in terms of the vocals and **instrumentals**, with good, solid **songwriting**. *Pyro* is a great **track** ▼: it's **catchy**, with beautiful **melodies** and **harmonies,** and I like the **lyrics**. But for me, the album lacks the **experimental** feel of their early music.'

WORD FOCUS

Music on CDs, records and downloads is produced as a **single** (= one song) or an **album** (= a collection of songs). One song on an album is called a **track**.

rhythm guitar a guitar style in which chords are played with a regular, repeated pattern.

lead vocalist the main singer in a group.

backing vocals singing that supports the main singer/vocalist in a group.

bass guitar an electric guitar that produces very low musical sounds.

lead guitar a guitar style that consists of mainly solos and tunes.

the charts PL N a weekly list showing the CDs that have sold the most copies.

award a prize given to sb for sth that they have achieved. **award sth** v.

number one the song or album that has sold the most copies that week.

record sth perform music so that it can be copied onto a CD, cassette, etc.

release sth make a CD, DVD, film, etc. available for people to see, hear or buy.

critic sb whose job is to write their opinions of music, films, books, etc.

polished of a very high quality.

instrumental part of a piece of music with instruments but no singing.

songwriting the process of writing songs.

catchy pleasing and easy to remember.

melody a sequence of musical notes that are nice to listen to; a tune.

harmony the pleasing way in which musical notes are played or sung together.

lyrics the words of a song.

experimental based on new ideas that are not yet proved to be successful.

Games and actions

ice hockey

stick

puck

He's about to pass the puck.

football

He's tackling another player.

tennis

racket

net

She's playing a forehand.

table tennis

bat

She's about to serve.

basketball

backboard

basket

He's about to shoot.

1 In ice hockey, you also *shoot* (= try to
  score a goal), but *tackle* is not used; in
  ice hockey tackling is called a (body)
  check.

2 In football, you also *shoot* (= try to
  score a goal), *pass* the ball, and head the
  ball (= hit the ball using your head).

3 In tennis, you play a backhand as well
  as a *forehand*. You also *serve* to begin
  a new point. In play, if you hit the ball
  before it touches the ground, it is a
  volley.

4 In table tennis you also play a
  forehand or *backhand*.

5 In basketball you also *pass* the ball,
  but *tackle* is not used; if you stop
  the progress of another player, it is
  called blocking.

Sports and equipment

He's putting /pʌtɪŋ/ to win the hole.

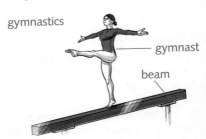

She's balancing on the beam.

She's competing in the slalom.

athletics

athlete

finishing line

He's about to win the race.

showjumping

rider

reins

saddle

fence

She's jumping a fence.

motor racing

chequered flag

crash helmet

He's about to win the race.

Football rules

In addition to the 11 players on the **pitch**, there may be five or six **substitutes,** although in most games only three of these can be used.

Once the game has started, the **referee** can **award** ▼ a **free kick** for a **foul**. For a bad foul such as a dangerous **tackle**, he may give a **yellow card** to a player or even a **red card**, which means that the player is **sent off**.

If a member of the **defending team commits a foul** ▼ in the **penalty area**, the **opposition** may be awarded a **penalty**, which is **taken** ▼ from the **penalty spot**.

The **offside** rule: a player is offside if they are in the **opponents'** half of the pitch, and they are in front of the ball, with only the opposition's goalkeeper between them and the goal.

WORD FOCUS

These verb + noun combinations are often used to talk about football.
The referee **gives** or **awards** (FML) a **free kick** or **penalty**.
A player **commits** a **foul**.
A player **takes** a **penalty**.
A player **scores** a **goal**.

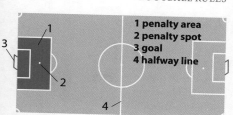

1 penalty area
2 penalty spot
3 goal
4 halfway line

pitch the area where you play the game.

substitute a player who replaces another player in a game.

referee the person who controls the game. He or she is helped by two linesmen.

free kick a team has a free kick if the other team does sth wrong.

foul (in sport) an action that is wrong and against the rules of the game. foul sb v.

tackle the act of trying to take the ball from an opponent. tackle sb v.

yellow card a card shown by the referee as a warning for a bad foul or bad behaviour. A red card means the player must leave the pitch.

send sb off order sb to leave the pitch because they have broken the rules.

defending team the team playing in their own half of the pitch. OPP attacking team.

the opposition the people, team, etc. that you are competing against.

penalty a chance to score with a direct free kick from the penalty spot.

opponent a person you are playing against in a game or competition.

A knockout cup

In the league, the winners are the best team over the whole season. But in a **knockout competition** ▼, luck plays a bigger part. Last year, we **were drawn** to play **at home** in the first **round** ▼ and won easily. After that we had to **play away** for the next two rounds, but we **got through**. Then, in the **quarter-final**, we were drawn against the **tournament** favourites. We **drew** one-**all** at their **ground**, but won the **replay** two-**nil**. As a result we were quite confident going into the **semi-final**, but we **were knocked out** by the team who went on to win the **trophy**. There was no **score** at the end of normal time, but they won one nil after **extra time**.

WORD FOCUS

A **competition** is an event in which players or teams **compete with** each other to find out who is the best. A **knockout competition** is one in which only the winning team or player in each **round** (= stage) continues to the next round.

A KNOCKOUT CUP

19.4

draw sb OFTEN PASSIVE choose sb to play against sb else by chance, e.g. by giving all the teams a number and then pulling numbers out of a bag in pairs.

at home if a team plays at home, they play in their own town. OPP (play) away.

get through (to sth) go forward to the next stage of a process, e.g. a competition.

quarter-final one of the four games that decide who plays in the semi-final, and then the final.

tournament a sports competition which is often played as a knockout competition.

draw if two teams draw, the scores are equal and neither side wins. draw N.

all used when the scores are equal; 2-2 is spoken as 'two all'.

ground an area of land used for a particular purpose: *a football ground*.

replay a game that is played again because no team won the previous game.

nil the number 0 in the result of a game.

knock sb out defeat sb so that they cannot continue competing. SYN eliminate sb.

trophy an object such as a silver cup that is given for winning a competition.

score the number of goals or points that a player/team has during a game. (The final score is the score at the end of the game.)

extra time a period of time that is added to the end of a game if there is no winner at the end of the normal period of time.

19.5

Sports leagues

How the league system works

In team sports such as football, ice hockey, or rugby, teams often play in a **league** competition. That means the teams usually play each other twice a **season**; once **at home** and once **away**. Teams usually prefer to play on their home **territory** because most of the **crowd** ▼ will be home **fans supporting** their own team and **cheering** them **on**; that gives them an advantage.

In many sports leagues around the world, the team that finishes **bottom** of the league is **relegated** to a lower **division** (sometimes more than one team). The team that finishes **top** are the **champions**, and they are **promoted** to a higher league, if there is one. In some leagues, the **runners-up** are also promoted.

WORD FOCUS

At a sports event, the **crowd** is the large number of people who come to watch it, e.g. *We had a crowd of 30,000 today.* People who watch an event, especially a sports event, are also called **spectators**. e.g. *A number of spectators ran onto the pitch at the end of the game.*

league a group of sports teams who all play each other to find which team is the best.

season a period of time during the year when a particular activity happens: *the football/hunting season*.

at home if a sports team plays at home, they play in the town where they come from. OPP away.

territory an area that a person or group considers as their own.

fan a sports fan is sb who likes watching a particular team or player.

support (a team) like a particular team and watch their matches. (People who do this are called supporters.)

cheer sb on shout loudly in order to encourage sb.

bottom the lowest level or position. OPP top.

relegate sb OFTEN PASSIVE (in sport) move a team from one league to a lower league. relegation N.

division one of the groups of football teams in a league, e.g. *the First/Second Division*.

champion(s) a person or team that has won a competition, especially in sport. (The competition is often called a championship, e.g. *the World Chess Championship*.)

promote sb OFTEN PASSIVE (in sport) move a team from one league to a higher league. promotion N.

runner(s)-up the person or team that finishes second in a competition.

Successful athletes

These are some of the **traits** that athletes need to **fulfil** their **potential**.

1 Commitment
Top performers are **determined** ▼ to succeed. Most people have **goals** in life, but top sportsmen and women tend to be very **single-minded**: they want to be the best and will **do everything in their power** to get there.

2 Self-belief
Others may **praise** you one moment and **criticize** you the next, but successful athletes always believe in themselves and their ability to achieve their goals.

3 Concentration
Top athletes know how to **maintain** their **focus** and **resist distractions**.

4 Toughness
Sportsmen and women all have **setbacks** – disappointments, injuries, etc., but the **toughest** athletes **overcome** them.

5 Dealing with emotions
Successful athletes are able to **channel** their emotions positively to **enhance** the level of their performance.

WORD FOCUS
If you are **determined**, you will not allow anything to stop you doing what you want to do. **determination** N.

trait a particular quality in your character.

fulfil sth do or achieve sth you hoped or
expected to do: *fulfil your potential/
ambition.*

potential abilities or qualities that exist and
can be developed further. SYN promise.

commitment an enthusiasm for
something and a determination to
succeed at it.

goal sth that you hope to achieve. SYN aim.

single-minded having your attention
fixed on only one thing.

do everything in your power = do
everything you possibly can.

praise sb say that sb has done sth very
well. praise N.

criticize sb/sth say what you do not like or
think is wrong with sb/sth. criticism N.

maintain sth keep sth at the same level.

focus the act of concentrating on one thing.

resist sth stop yourself from doing sth that
you would like to do.

distraction sth that gets your attention and
stops you concentrating on sth else.

toughness the strength to deal with difficult
conditions or situations. tough ADJ.

setback a problem that delays or stops
progress, or makes a situation worse.
set sb back V.

overcome sth succeed in dealing with or
controlling a problem.

channel sth direct feelings, ideas, etc.
towards one particular purpose.

enhance sth improve the quality of sth.

Why education?

We still have high levels of **illiteracy**, **truancy** is **rife**, and many young people think school is a waste of time. But it shouldn't be.

It is **proven** that a good education will improve children's **prospects,** and **open doors** that might otherwise be closed. It will increase their chance of finding a good job, and with it the **likelihood** of more money and higher **status**. But a good education should be more than that. It should help children to develop **self-esteem** ▼ and **self-awareness** ▼. It should teach them to **take responsibility for** the world they **inhabit**, so they understand why they **vote** in elections, why **freedom of speech** is important, why **preventive** health care **matters**, etc.

Education should also help children to unlock their **innate capacity** to be creative. Finally, it should teach them to have respect for other **human beings** and give them a sense of **morality**.

WORD FOCUS

Self- is often combined with other nouns and adjectives to mean 'of yourself': **self-esteem** is the feeling of being happy with your own character; **self-awareness** is a knowledge and understanding of yourself.

illiteracy the inability to read or write.
    illiterate ADJ, OPP literate.

truancy the practice of staying away from
    school without permission. Someone
    who does this is playing truant.

rife (of bad or unpleasant things) very
    common: *corruption is rife*. SYN
    widespread.

proven tested and shown to be true.

prospects PL N the chances of being
    successful in the future.

open doors give sb opportunities.

likelihood the chance of sth happening.
    SYN probability.

status your social or professional position.

take responsibility for sth make decisions
    and accept the consequences if they are
    wrong.

inhabit sth live in a particular place.

vote (for sb/sth) choose sb/sth by
    marking a paper or raising your hand.

freedom of speech the right to say what
    you want without anyone stopping you.

preventive (also preventative) intended
    to stop sth that causes problems from
    happening.

matter be important.

innate (of a quality, feeling, etc.) that you
    have when you are born.

capacity to do sth ability to do sth.

human being a living person.

morality the principles of right or
    wrong behaviour.

20.2

School issues

In the UK, there is a continuing **debate** about many **issues regarding** the education of our children. For example:

- At the age of two or three, **is a child better off** in a **nursery school** with other children, or at home with their mother or **childminder**?

- Are **independent**▼ schools **divisive** and **elitist**, or do parents have the right to send their children to fee-paying **private schools**▼ with smaller class sizes, and **statistically** a much higher chance of getting into university?

- There is some evidence that girls do well in single-sex schools where they are not **being distracted by** boys. If that is true, are **co-educational** schools still better than single-sex schools?

- Should religion be a **compulsory** subject on the **curriculum**? And if so, what should we be teaching?

- How should we **tackle bullying** in schools?

WORD FOCUS

An **independent school** receives no money from the government, and the education of the pupils is paid for by the parents. SYN **private school**. OPP **state school**.

debate an argument or discussion expressing different opinions.

issue an important topic that people are discussing.

regarding sth/sb about sth/sb. SYN concerning sth/sb.

be better off (doing sth) used to say that sb would be happier or more satisfied if they did a particular thing. OPP be worse off.

nursery school a school for children between the ages of about two and five.

childminder a person who is paid to care for children while their parents are at work.

divisive likely to cause arguments between people.

elitist based on a system in which a small group of people (= an elite) have a lot of advantages and have the most influence.

statistically based on information shown in numbers. statistics N.

be distracted by sth have your concentration interrupted by sth.

co-educational (co-ed INF) educating boys and girls in the same school.

compulsory if sth is compulsory, you have to do it. SYN obligatory.

curriculum the group of subjects that students study at school or college.

tackle sth make a big effort to deal with a difficult situation: *tackle a problem*.

bullying behaviour that frightens or hurts sb smaller and weaker. The person is a bully.

20.3 Discipline

Has discipline got worse?

Discipline ▼ is often **cited** as one of the biggest problems in schools, and these are some of the reasons that people give:

- The **abolition** of **corporal punishment** has removed a common **deterrent** to bad behaviour.
- Rules are not consistently **enforced**, and some teachers **ignore misconduct**.
- Head teachers are frightened to **suspend** or **expel disruptive** students in case the students or their parents take legal action against them.
- Parents **are to blame for** not **disciplining ▼** their children at home.
- **Gang** culture, common in society, is spreading into schools, creating more violence and discipline problems.
- Poor teaching **results in** a **deterioration** in classroom behaviour.
- Children in general have lost **respect** for people **in authority**.

WORD FOCUS

Discipline is the practice of making people **obey** rules (= do what the rules say), and then **punishing** them (= making them suffer) if they don't. We also use **discipline** as a verb: *Parents have to discipline their children.*

cite sth FML give sth as a reason or example to support what you are saying.

abolition the ending of a law, a system, or an institution. abolish sth v.

corporal punishment the physical punishment of sb by hitting them.

deterrent sth that, because it is unpleasant, makes sb decide not to do sth. deter sb v.

enforce sth make people follow a particular law or rule. enforcement N.

ignore sth pay no attention to sth.

misconduct bad or unacceptable behaviour.

suspend sb (from sth) officially stop a student from going to school, or a person from going to work, for a period of time.

expel sb (from sth) officially make sb leave a school or organization.

disruptive causing problems, noise, etc. so that sth cannot continue normally. disrupt sth v.

be to blame for sth be responsible for sth bad.

gang a group of young people who spend time together and often cause trouble.

result in sth cause sth to happen.

deterioration a situation in which sth becomes worse. deteriorate v.

respect a feeling of admiration for sb because of their status or importance.

in authority having a position of power to give orders to people.

20.4 Exam revision

Here are some **tips** for exam **revision**.

- The first **step** is to **draw up** a revision **schedule**. Be **realistic**. You can't **revise** all the time.

- Consider how long you can concentrate at any one time. **There's no point in▼** sitting in front of your notes for hours if you're not **absorbing** anything. It is probably wiser to revise **in short bursts**.

- Taking short breaks in your revision periods can be really **beneficial**. For one thing, it allows time for ideas and information to **sink in**.

- There won't be enough time to do everything, so **prioritize** your revision. Which topics are **bound to come up** and therefore essential to revise?

- When you've **come up with** a timetable, it's important to realize that things will not always **go according to plan**. Be ready to reorganize your schedule and your **priorities** to make sure you **stay on track**.

WORD FOCUS

Point can mean the purpose or aim of something. It is often used in these ways:
There's no point in trying to do it all.
What's the point of revising everything?
I don't see the point of exams.

tip a small piece of advice about sth.

revision the process of preparing for an exam by looking again at the work you have done. **revise (for sth)** v.

step one of a series of things that you do in order to achieve sth.

draw sth up make or write sth that needs careful thought: *draw up a plan*.

schedule a plan of activities or events and when they will happen.

realistic sensible and accepting things as they are.

absorb sth take information into your mind and understand or remember it.

in short bursts in short periods in which you do sth with a lot of energy or effort.

beneficial (to sth/sb) improving a situation or having a helpful or useful effect.

sink in (of words, information, etc.) be fully understood.

prioritize sth put tasks, problems, etc. in order of importance so that you deal with the most important first. **priority** N.

bound to do sth be certain to do sth or happen.

come up happen or appear.

come up with sth find or produce an answer, a plan, a sum of money, etc.

go according to plan happen in the way that you expect.

stay on track keep going in the right direction, or doing the right things.

University

Sussex is a campus university. I lived on campus in a hall of residence.	A campus university is one where all the university buildings are situated on one site: *on campus.* hall of residence a building for university students to live in.
I had to pay tuition fees.	the money that you pay to be taught.
Some students got a grant.	a sum of money given by the government or other organization for a particular purpose.
My best friend managed to get a scholarship.	a sum of money given to sb by an organization to help pay for their education.
There are over 10,000 undergraduates.	students studying for a first degree.
I was in the faculty of social sciences.	a department or group of related departments in a university.
My brother did a degree in history.	a university course, usually lasting three years or more. If you successfully complete the course, you have a degree in sth.

We had about 12 lectures each week.

a talk that is given to a group of people, who listen and often take notes. A lecturer is a class at university where a lecturer and a small group of students discuss a topic.

We had a tutorial three times a term.

A tutorial is a class at university involving discussion between an individual student or a small group, and a tutor (= a lecturer with responsibility for certain students). A term is a period of time when students are attending university. There are normally three terms in a year.

I passed my finals.

the last exams taken by university students at the end of their final year. If you pass them, you graduate. (see below)

I graduated nearly ten years ago. My degree was in Psychology.

graduate v /ˈɡrædʒueɪt/ leave university with a degree. A person is then a graduate /ˈɡrædʒuət/.

20.6 Postgraduate courses

Postgraduate courses in Education

Qualifications and duration
MA (FT 1 year; PT 2-5 years)
Postgraduate Diploma in Education (PDE)
(FT 9 months; PT 2-5 years)

Overview
90 **credits** are required for the MA: 60 credits from taught **modules** and 30 credits for a 15,000 word **dissertation** ▼. Students who **opt for** the PDE require 60 credits. A unit on research methods in education (12 credits) is compulsory on both courses.

Students can **specialize in** a particular area or combine units in different areas. Units are available in various **modes** of study, including taught modules as well as a **distance learning** programme.

Entry requirements
A first degree or **equivalent** from a **recognized** university.

WORD FOCUS

A **dissertation** is a long piece of writing, e.g. 10,000 words, on a particular subject, often for a university degree. It is usually longer than an **essay**, e.g. 500 words, but shorter than a **thesis**, e.g. 60,000 words.

qualification OFTEN PLURAL sth such as a degree or diploma that you get when you successfully finish a course of study.

duration the length of time sth continues.

MA (ABBREV Master of Arts) a higher degree in an arts subject. (Also MSc. ABBREV Master of Science.)

postgraduate (postgrad INF) a person who already has a first degree and who is doing advanced study or research.

diploma a qualification at the end of a course of study at a college or university.

overview a general description of sth.

credit a part of a college or university course that you have completed successfully.

module a unit that forms part of a course of study at college or university.

opt for sth choose sth.

specialize in sth spend more time on one area of work, and become very knowledgeable in that area.

mode a particular way of doing sth.

distance learning a system of education in which people study at home with the help of the internet and videos, and then send or email their work to their teachers.

entry requirement a qualification or experience that you need in order to enter a college or university.

equivalent equal in value, meaning, etc.

recognize sth if sth is recognized, it is officially approved of and accepted.

20.7 University of the Third Age

The University of the Third Age, usually **referred to as** the U3A, was **founded** in France as part of the University of Toulouse in the 1970s. Its aim was to provide educational, creative and leisure opportunities for **retired** people.

U3As quickly **spread** all over the world. In the British model, U3As have no connection with universities, but are **autonomous self-help** groups run by the **voluntary** ▼ efforts of the members. The word 'university' is used in its **original** sense of people coming together to **pursue** learning in all its forms.

The courses and activities offered are those that **reflect** the **wishes** of its members, and are all run by the members for free, **utilizing** their **vast** body of knowledge and **expertise** gained over a **lifetime**. There is a small **subscription** to join, but after that courses are usually free, **thus** making the U3A **affordable** and **accessible** to all.

WORD FOCUS

If something is **voluntary**, people do it because they want to do it, not because they have to do it. If people **volunteer** to do something, they are **volunteers.**

refer to sth/sb as sth call or describe sth/
    sb as sth.

found sth OFTEN PASSIVE start an
    organization, political party, etc.

retired no longer working because you have
    reached a particular age, e.g. 60 or 65.

spread (PT, PP spread) become known or
    used by more and more people.

autonomous (of a country, organization,
    etc.) able to control its own affairs.

self-help relying on your own efforts
    to do sth, without depending on
    other people.

original first; earliest.

pursue sth follow a course or activity.

reflect sth show or be a sign of sth.

wish a thing that you want to have or to
    happen.

utilize sth FML use sth. SYN make use of sth.

vast extremely large in area, amount, etc.

expertise special knowledge or skill in a
    particular subject. (The person is an
    expert.)

lifetime the period of time when sb is alive.

subscription an amount of money you
    pay, usually once a year, to be a member
    of sth, or receive sth such as a magazine.

thus FML as a result of sth just mentioned.
    SYNS hence FML, therefore.

affordable if sth is affordable, you have
    enough money to pay for it. afford sth v.

accessible if sth is accessible, it can be
    easily used, reached, seen, etc.

21.1

Writing an essay

Whatever type of **essay** ▼ you have to write, e.g. **description**, **narrative**, **comparison**, or **argument**, begin by **jotting down** ideas on paper. At this stage, it isn't important in what order you write your ideas – just put down anything that you think is **relevant**.

When you have done that, you can start to plan the essay. **Build up** an **outline** of what you want to say in each **paragraph** ▼. Make sure the ideas are **coherent**, and relevant to the essay title. Don't **wander off the subject** or **waffle**.

You can now write your first **draft**. When you have finished, **read** it **through** and make any necessary **revisions**. Finally, **proofread** the essay to make sure you haven't made any **careless** spelling, punctuation or grammar mistakes.

WORD FOCUS

A paragraph is a section of a piece of writing, usually consisting of several sentences on a single subject. In an **essay** (= a short piece of writing on a particular subject), you usually have an **opening/introductory paragraph**, several paragraphs for the main part of the essay, then a **final paragraph** at the end.

description a piece of writing that tells you what sth or sb is like. describe sth v.

narrative a story of sth that has happened.

comparison the process of considering how two things or people are similar or different. compare A with/to B v.

argument a reason or reasons that sb uses to show that sth is true or correct. argue for/against sth v.

jot sth down write sth quickly.

relevant (to sth) directly connected with or important to what is being discussed.

build sth up create and develop sth.

outline a description of the general points about sth but not the details. outline sth v.

coherent (of ideas, thoughts, etc.) logical, well-organized, and clear. OPP incoherent.

wander off the subject move away from the subject that you should be discussing.

waffle INF use a lot of words without saying anything interesting or important.

draft a piece of writing, e.g. an essay, that is not in its final form.

read sth through read sth carefully from beginning to end.

revision a change, addition or improvement to sth. revise sth v.

proofread sth read and correct a piece of written or printed work.

careless resulting from a lack of thought or attention.

21.2

Essay titles

You need to understand key words that are commonly used in essay titles.

Distinguish the main sources of energy and **evaluate** their importance.

Analyse ▼ the changes in American foreign policy since 1945.

Examine ▼ the **role** of destiny in 'Romeo and Juliet'.

Define what you understand by 'postmodernism', and **discuss** ▼ its role in late twentieth century architecture.

Compare life before and after the introduction of personal computers.

Account for the increase in asthma in the last forty years.

List the **criteria** you would use to **assess** the strength of a business.

What **factors determine** the way people spend their income?

Summarize the **benefits** of a free national health service. **Illustrate** your answer with examples.

WORD FOCUS

If you are asked to **analyse, examine** or **discuss** a particular subject in an essay, you have to write about it in detail, and show you understand different aspects of it, e.g. its advantages and disadvantages.

distinguish sth recognize the differences between things: *I can't distinguish one type of oil from another.*

evaluate sth form an opinion of the value or quality of sth after thinking about it carefully. N evaluation. SYN assess sth V, assessment N.

role the purpose or influence of sb or sth in a particular situation: *Destiny plays a crucial/decisive/major role in the plot of 'Romeo and Juliet'.*

define sth explain the meaning of sth. definition N.

compare A with/to B say how two things are similar or different. (Also make a comparison between two things.)

account for sth give an explanation of sth. SYN explain sth.

criterion SING (criteria PL) a standard or principle that is used to judge sth or make a decision about sth.

factor one of several things that cause or influence sth.

determine sth make sth happen in a particular way.

summarize sth give a short account of the main facts or features of sth. summary N.

benefit a helpful and useful effect that sth has. beneficial ADJ.

illustrate sth make the meaning of sth clearer by using examples. illustration N.

21.3 Linking ideas

Roads speed ahead

The government seems to be committed to a new road-building programme, which could cost an estimated £4 billion. **Moreover**, they plan to spend extra money on improving the state of existing roads in and around major cities.

In a speech last night, Transport Secretary, Liam Knight, said that **in contrast with** the rail network which had received significant funding over the last ten years, the roads were badly in need of radical improvement.

Needless to say, the plan has come under fierce attack from environmental groups. They believe that **in addition to** the escalating cost, further road building would **lead to** more cars on the roads and **consequently** higher levels of pollution. Liam Knight denies this. **In fact**, he has argued that **in spite of** rising numbers of cars on the road, pollution levels will fall **due to** the lower emissions from modern cars, and the emergence of electric cars over the next ten years. This is unlikely to appease the green lobby, who are organizing a series of protests against the plans. **Nevertheless**, the government seems determined to press ahead. ∎

moreover used to introduce a second fact or reason that supports what you have just said. SYNS in addition, furthermore, what's more MAINLY SPOKEN.

in/by contrast (with sth) used when you are comparing things and saying that the second thing is very different from the first.

needless to say used to say that sth is already known or understood. SYN it goes without saying (that ...) MAINLY SPOKEN.

in addition (to sth) used when you want to say that sth extra exists or is happening together with the thing that you are talking about. SYN as well as (sth).

lead to sth cause sth. SYN result in sth.

consequently because of sth just mentioned. SYNS as a result, therefore, thus FML.

in (actual) fact used to emphasize a statement, especially one that is the opposite of what has just been said.

in spite of sth used to say that sth happens although sth else might have stopped it. SYN despite sth.

due to sth/sb because of sth/sb.

nevertheless in spite of a fact or idea you have just mentioned. This word is used to show how a new idea is related to what has just been said.

21.4

Adding interest

Using a range of adjectives – not the same common ones all the time – can make an essay more interesting. For example, instead of describing a book or film as *interesting* or *exciting*, you could say it was **fascinating**, **gripping**, **absorbing**, **engaging** or **stimulating**.

Here are some more examples:

We had ~~terrible~~ weather. (**dreadful**, **appalling**, or **atrocious** weather).

It was a ~~fantastic~~ concert. (a **superb**, a **brilliant**, or an **outstanding** concert).

The room was very ~~nice~~. (**elegant**, **stylish**, **classy** or **impressive**).

I thought his behaviour was a bit ~~strange~~. (**bizarre**, **weird**, **peculiar**, or **odd**).

It was a ~~horrible~~ attack. (a **cruel** ▼, **violent**, **vicious** or **brutal** attack).

WORD FOCUS

Some of the words above are synonyms, or similar in meaning, but there are certain contexts where we prefer one word rather than another, e.g. a *brutal murder*; a *vicious dog* (= aggressive or dangerous); a *vicious temper* (= getting angry very quickly and in an aggressive and unpleasant way); a *cruel remark* (= a comment that hurts sb).

fascinating extremely interesting.

gripping interesting or exciting in a way that keeps your attention. SYN absorbing.

engaging interesting or pleasant in a way that keeps your attention.

stimulating ideas that make you feel enthusiastic or excited about sth.

dreadful very bad or unpleasant. SYN awful INF.

appalling very bad or shocking (often used about accidents, crimes, or social conditions).

atrocious very bad or unpleasant (often used about weather).

superb extremely good. SYN brilliant.

outstanding excellent (often used about effort and achievement).

elegant attractive and showing a good sense of style. SYN stylish.

classy INF expensive and/or fashionable.

impressive if sth is impressive, you admire it and like it because it is very good and of high quality.

bizarre very strange or unusual. SYN weird.

peculiar very strange or unusual, especially when it is unpleasant or worrying. SYN odd.

cruel sb who is cruel enjoys causing pain to others, or making them unhappy and upset.

violent using physical force with the intention of causing damage or injury.

vicious extremely violent. SYN brutal.

21.5 Avoiding repetition

We generally try to avoid repeating the same word in a sentence, e.g. *I didn't share his **opinion**, but it was an interesting **opinion**.* This would read better as: *I didn't share his **opinion**, but it was an interesting **point of view**.*

Here are more ways to avoid repetition by using synonyms or near synonyms.

Lucy didn't **appreciate**▼ how ill he was, but when she saw him, she **realized**▼ that it was very serious.

Most of the **findings** from the survey showed the **results** to be inconclusive.

Despite the **advances** made in various cancer treatments, there is limited **progress** in other areas of medicine.

He **achieved** a great deal at first, but has **accomplished** little in recent years.

Avoid the city centre at night, and always **steer clear of** the bus station.

The lawyer **misrepresented** what Jacobs said and totally **distorted** the facts.

After the **disastrous** floods last year, another year of rain would be a **catastrophe** for the region.

The article made a number of **remarks** about the service, but didn't **comment on** the food at all.

point of view a person's opinion.

appreciate sth understand that sth is true.
SYN realize sth.

findings PL N information learned as a
result of research. SYN results.

advance a development in science,
technology, human knowledge, etc.

achieve sth successfully do or complete
sth, especially after working hard at it.
SYN accomplish sth.

avoid sth keep away from sth. SYN steer
clear of sth.

misrepresent sth/sb give the wrong
information about sth/sb so that other
people have the wrong impression
about them.

distort sth change a fact or idea, so that it
is no longer correct or true.

disastrous very bad and harmful.
SYN catastrophic.

catastrophe a sudden event that
causes harm, suffering, damage, etc.
SYN disaster.

remark sth you say or write which gives
your opinion or thought. SYN comment.

comment (on sth) express an opinion
about sth. SYN remark.

WORD FOCUS

These pairs of words are synonyms
in some senses or contexts, but not
others, e.g. I **realized** I'd seen her
before. (NOT ~~appreciated~~); I really
appreciate your help. (NOT ~~realize~~).

21.6

Writing a CV

If you have to write a **CV** ▼, make it no longer than two pages, and make sure it looks attractive, **professional** and easy to read. If you **apply for** different jobs or courses, be prepared to **adapt** your CV so that it is **appropriate** for what you are applying for. Include **the following**:

- **Personal details**: name, address, phone, email.
- **Profile**: be positive, but don't **boast**.
- Education: secondary schools, colleges and universities **attended**. Put the most recent details first.
- **Qualifications**: give the British **equivalent** of your qualifications if you can.
- Work experience: recent details first.
- **Skills**: e.g. languages spoken, a driving licence, web page design skills.
- **Interests**: try to be **specific**, e.g. 'I am a member of a drama company.' Avoid **vague** hobbies such as reading or films.
- **References**: give the names, titles and addresses of two **referees**.

WORD FOCUS

CV is an abbreviation of **curriculum vitae** (= a written record of your education and experience when you are applying for a job). In American English it is called a **résumé**.

professional done in the correct way and showing skill and ability.

apply for sth make a formal request in writing for a job or course. application N.

adapt sth make changes to sth so that it is suitable for a particular purpose.

appropriate suitable, acceptable or correct for the situation. OPP inappropriate.

the following the thing or things that you will mention next.

personal details information about yourself.

profile a detailed description of yourself.

boast (about sth) speak too proudly about what you have done or what you own.

attend sth RATHER FML spend time at a school, university, event, etc.

qualification sth such as a degree or diploma which you receive when you successfully finish a course of study.

equivalent (of/to sth) sth that is equal in value, amount, meaning or importance to sth else. equivalent ADJ.

skill an ability, e.g. being able to drive, speaking a language, etc.

interest an activity or subject you enjoy.

specific exact and detailed.

vague not giving enough information about sth.

reference a letter by sb who knows you, giving information about your character and abilities, especially to a new employer.

referee sb who writes a reference for you.

21.7

Personal statements

Many universities ask **prospective** students to **accompany** their **application** with a *personal statement*. This is an opportunity for you to tell the university why you are suitable to do a particular course, and to **demonstrate** your **enthusiasm** and **commitment**. Here are some important **dos and don'ts**:

- Do check university and college **prospectuses** ▼ and websites, as they usually tell you the **criteria** for acceptance and qualities they want students to demonstrate.

- Do expect to write several **drafts** before you are satisfied.

- Do ask people to give you **feedback**.

- Don't lie. If you **exaggerate**, you may **get caught out** at an interview.

- Don't use **elaborate** language. Keep your English simple and **coherent**.

- Don't **leave it till the last minute**. Your statement will seem **rushed** and important information may be **left out**.

See page 32 for examples.

> **WORD FOCUS**
>
> A **prospectus** is a book that gives information about a school, university, etc. in order to advertise it. A **brochure** gives information about holidays, etc.

prospective expected to do sth or
become sth.

accompany sth appear with sth else.

application a formal (often written)
request for sth, e.g. a job or course.

demonstrate sth show sth clearly.

enthusiasm a strong feeling of excitement
and interest in sth. enthusiastic ADJ.

commitment willingness to give time and
energy to sth. committed ADJ.

dos and don'ts a list of things you must
or must not do.

criterion (PL criteria) a standard or
principle by which sth is judged or
decided.

draft a piece of writing that may have later
changes made to it before it is finished.

feedback advice or criticism about how
sb has done sth, or how useful sth is.

exaggerate sth make sth seem larger,
better, worse or more important than it
really is. exaggeration N.

catch sb out OFTEN PASSIVE make sb do
or say sth in order to prove that they are
lying or do not know sth.

elaborate very complicated and detailed.

coherent (of ideas, thoughts, etc.) logical,
well organized, and clear.

leave sth till the last minute do sth at the
latest possible time.

rushed done too quickly.

leave sth out not include sth. SYN omit
sth FML.

Formal letters

These words and phrases are commonly used in formal letters.

Dear Sir/Madam ▼

I am writing
- to **inform you that** …
- to **enquire about** …
- to **complain about** …
- **in response to** …
- **regarding** …

I regret to inform you that we cannot …

I would like to **apologize for** the delay.

Further to
- your letter **of** 7 May, …
- our conversation today, …

With reference to your letter of 2 June,

I would be grateful if you could send …

I **am enclosing** a copy of …

If you **require further details, please do not hesitate to contact me.**

I look forward to hearing from you.

Yours faithfully ▼
Kristen Campbell
Kristen Campbell

> ## WORD FOCUS
>
> Use **Dear Sir/Madam** if you do not know the person's name, and end the letter with **Yours faithfully**. Use the person's name if you know it, and end the letter with **Yours sincerely**.

inform sb (that) give sb information about sth.

enquire (about sth) ask sb for information (about sth). Also spelt inquire.

complain (about sth) say that you are unhappy or not satisfied with sth.

in response to sth/sb in reply to sth/sb.

regarding about. SYN concerning.

I regret to inform you (that) = I am sorry to tell you (that).

apologize (for sth) say you are sorry for sth.

further to sth FML used to show that you are referring to a previous letter or conversation.

of (7 May) = dated (the 7th of May), or written on the 7th of May.

with reference to sth FML used to say what you are talking or writing about.

I would be grateful if you could … commonly used to make a polite request for sth.

enclose sth if you enclose sth with a letter, you include sth with the letter. Also Please find enclosed …

require sth FML need sth.

further details more information.

please do not hesitate to contact me = I am very happy for you to write to, phone or email me.

I look forward to hearing from you commonly used at the end of a letter when you are expecting a reply.

22.1

A descriptive essay

> *Write a description of your town or city*
> *for someone who has never been there.*

I have lived in Baden-Baden all my life. It
is a **sophisticated, cosmopolitan** town,
situated on the **banks** of the River Oos,
at the foot of the Black Forest in south-
west Germany.

Originally, the Romans made use of
its natural hot **springs**, and by the 18th
century, it was famous as a **spa resort**.
(Baden means 'bathe' in German.)

Baden-Baden is also **renowned for** its
diverse cultural activities–museums,
art galleries and concert halls–as well
as being very **picturesque**. It has the
Lichtentaler Allee, a **massive** park with
an avenue **running** through the middle,
where people can **stroll** throughout the
year. The park is also where you will find
the *Spielbank*–the oldest **casino** ▼ in
Germany. Baden-Baden has a **thriving**
gambling ▼ industry in addition to its
beautiful parks, elegant streets, and
many boutiques.

WORD FOCUS

Gambling is an activity in which you
risk losing money in order to win more,
e.g. roulette. A **casino** is a place where
people **gamble**.

sophisticated offering cultural activities, fashionable shops and restaurants, etc.

cosmopolitan including people from many different countries and cultures.

situated found in a particular place. SYN located.

bank the area of land along the side of a river: *on the bank of the river Severn.*

foot the bottom of a mountain, hill, set of stairs, etc.: *The town is at the foot of the mountain.*

originally at the beginning; at first.

spring a flow of water from under the ground, forming a stream (= a small river) or pool.

spa a place with a natural supply of mineral water which is often considered good for your health.

resort a place where a lot of people go on holiday.

renowned for (doing) sth famous or admired for a special achievement.

diverse varied; different from each other.

picturesque (of a place or scene) very attractive, especially because it is old and interesting.

massive very large.

run if a road or path runs somewhere, it passes along or through it.

stroll walk in a casual way. stroll N.

thriving very successful. thrive V.

22.2

A discursive essay

> *Cars should be **banned** ▼ from all city centres. Discuss.*

As car **ownership** increases, city centres are becoming more and more **congested**: parking spaces are no longer **adequate**, and rush hour traffic **brings** cities **to a standstill**. It is **inevitable**, therefore, that we will have to **restrict** the number of cars in city centres. **In addition**, cars cause **pollution**, which is **damaging** not only for people's health, but also for old buildings in **historic** city centres.

Many people, **however**, are **dependent on** their cars to travel to and from work. **Consequently**, if we are going to ban them from city centres, we have to provide **commuters** with a cheap and **efficient** public transport system, at least within the city, and only allow taxis to move around the centre. Without these things, we cannot expect motorists to **give up** their cars.

In an ideal world it seems sensible to ban private cars from city centres, but **in practice** it may be difficult.

WORD FOCUS

If you **ban** sth, you say officially that sth must not be done, sold or used. SYN **prohibit sth. ban** N.

ownership the fact of possessing sth, usually sth big and valuable.

congested crowded; full of traffic. **congestion** N.

adequate enough in quantity or quality.

bring sth to a standstill cause a situation in which sth cannot move or happen.

inevitable impossible to avoid or prevent.

restrict sth limit the amount, size, etc. of sth.

in addition used to mention another person or thing.

pollution the process of allowing dirty or harmful substances to enter the air, rivers, etc. **pollute sth** V.

damaging having a bad effect on sth/sb.

historic old, interesting, and important in history.

however used to introduce a statement that contrasts with sth that has just been said.

dependent on sth/sb needing sth/sb in order to live or succeed.

consequently as a result; therefore.

commuter sb who travels into a city every day for work. **commuting** N.

efficient working well and producing good results. OPP **inefficient**.

give sth up stop using or doing sth.

in an ideal world used for saying what should be true in a perfect world, although that is not likely to happen.

in practice used to talk about what really happens, not what should happen.

22.3

A report

You recently attended an English language course. Write a report for the school giving your views on the course to help them plan future courses.

My **overall impression** of the school is **as follows**:

Positive **features**:
- The teachers were all **well qualified**, hard-working and very **supportive**.
- The **atmosphere** was very friendly.
- The **facilities** were excellent.

Points to consider:
- Some classrooms were a bit **cramped**.
- The food in the school **canteen** was **decent**, but it **lacked** variety, and the lunch break was not long enough if you wanted to go out for lunch.
- Some of the students were lazy and **reluctant** to do homework. This **held back** the progress of other students.
- There weren't many organized social activities.

Recommendations:
- Improve the food in the canteen or **extend** the lunch break.
- Make homework **compulsory**.
- Increase the number of social activities.

overall general; including everything.

impression an idea, feeling or opinion that you have about sth/sb: *a(n) good/bad/ general/overall impression.*

as follows used when you are going to give more details about sth.

feature an important part or aspect of sth.

qualified having passed the exams or completed the training needed to do a particular job: *well/highly qualified.*

supportive helpful and sympathetic.

atmosphere the feeling or mood that exists in a place.

facilities the buildings, equipment, etc. which are provided for a particular purpose.

point an aspect or feature.

cramped (of a room) not having enough space for the people in it.

canteen a place in a school, factory, etc. where food and drink are served.

decent good or good enough.

lack sth not have enough of sth. **lack** N.

reluctant (to do sth) not wanting to do sth. SYN unwilling.

hold sb back prevent the progress or development of sb.

recommendation a piece of advice about what to do in a particular situation.

extend sth make sth bigger or longer.

compulsory if sth is compulsory, you have to do it. SYN obligatory. OPP optional.

22.4

A story

Write a story beginning with the words, "I had never felt so nervous in my life!"

I had never felt so nervous in my life! I was about to stand up and perform a **solo** in a competition for **choirs** from all over the country. I'd found the solo really difficult, and seriously wondered whether I **was up to** it.

When the day arrived, I **had butterflies in my stomach** throughout the journey to the concert hall, and **by the time** we took to the stage I was absolutely **petrified**. The choir all sang together for the first part of the performance, and then it was my **turn** – my solo. My legs were **trembling** as I started, but the **conductor** gave me a big smile; that made me feel a bit better. Gradually I started to **grow in confidence**, and even began to enjoy the sound coming out of my mouth.

Finally it was over. The rest of the choir **joined in**, and I **breathed a sigh of relief**. Someone behind **congratulated** me, which was nice. And when we finished, the audience response was amazing. They kept **clapping**, and I had to step forward and **take a bow**. It was the proudest moment of my life.

solo a piece of music, dance or entertainment performed by one person.

choir a group of people who sing together, e.g. in a church or school.

be up to sth be good enough to do sth.

have/get butterflies in your stomach feel very nervous about sth you are going to do.

by the time used to say what has already happened at the time that sth else happens.

petrified extremely frightened.

turn a time when one person in a group can or must do sth, before or after sb else.

tremble make small, quick movements of the body from fear, excitement or cold.

conductor the person who stands in front of an orchestra or choir and leads them.

grow in sth begin to have more of a particular quality: *grow in confidence/ popularity.*

join in (with sb) start to do an activity with others who are already doing it.

breathe a sigh of relief breathe a long, slow breath out, indicating a relaxed, happy feeling because sth has ended.

congratulate sb tell sb you are pleased for them because they have done sth well.

clap hit your hands together repeatedly to show that you like sth. SYN applaud.

take a bow make a forward movement of the top part of your body at the end of a performance to thank the audience. **bow** v.

An article

How have eating habits changed in your country in the last thirty years?

Eating habits in the UK have changed a great deal in the last thirty years, and not always **for the better**. The main problem is that **nowadays** many people rely on **convenience food rather than** cooking fresh food, and a lot of young people **consume** too much of the **junk food** you get in **fast food** restaurants.

On the other hand, there is a growing **awareness** of food and how it **contributes to** good health. For example, more people are eating butter or drinking milk with a reduced fat **content**. The demand for **organic food** is also increasing, and local farmers' markets are **springing up** everywhere, providing people with local food **in season**, which reduces **food miles**.

A significant change with more **migration** and more foreign holidays is that people's diets have become more **diverse**. Italian pasta, Indian curry and French cheese are now an everyday part of our diet, and increasingly, people are **eating out** a lot more than they did in the past.

for the better if sth changes for the better,
it improves. OPP for the worse.

nowadays at the present time.

convenience food food that is ready-
prepared or frozen and is quick and
easy to prepare.

rather than used for saying that one thing
is preferred to another.

consume sth FML eat or drink sth.

junk food food that is unhealthy because
it contains too much fat, sugar, etc.

fast food food that is made and served
quickly, often to be eaten as a takeaway.

on the other hand used to introduce a
different opinion.

awareness knowledge or understanding
of a subject, issue, situation, etc.

contribute (to sth) help make sth happen.

content the amount of a substance that
sth contains: *high sugar content/low fat
content.*

organic (of food) produced naturally
without using artificial chemicals.

spring up appear suddenly and quickly.

in season fruit and vegetables that are
in season are growing now, in large
amounts.

food miles the distance food travels from
where it is produced to where it is eaten.

migration the process of people moving
to work or live permanently in other
countries.

diverse varied; different from each other.

eat out eat in a restaurant. OPP eat in.

22.6

An informal letter

You have received this message:

Duncan, I'm planning to come and do an English course in London. What advice can you give me?
Cheers, Hakan.

Write a letter in reply.

Dear Hakan

I'm **delighted** to **hear** you're planning to do a course here in London. **As you know**, your English is great already, but you'll still make **loads of** progress in **a relatively short space of time**. **I'd be inclined to go for** a fairly **intensive** course (**somewhere in the region of** 20 hours a week), and **preferably** with a maximum of 12 students in a class. **Given** your background, you should also be looking for a course with some business **content**.

As far as accommodation **is concerned**, **your best bet** is to stay with an English family – you'll get more speaking practice. I'd **put** you **up** at our place, but it's impossible now we've just had the baby.

I'll be **tied up** at work during the day, but we can **get together** in the evenings, and Emily's **thrilled** you're coming.

Let me know what you decide to do.

All the best, Duncan.

delighted very happy, especially because sth good has happened.

hear sth be told sth.

as you know used when you are saying sth that sb already knows.

loads of sth INF a lot of sth.

relatively to a significant degree (compared with other things): *relatively short/easy*, etc.

a short space of time a short period of time.

I'd be inclined to (do sth) = I suggest that you (do sth) (used to give advice).

go for sth choose sth.

intensive involving a lot of work or activity in a short period of time.

(somewhere) in the region of about; approximately.

preferably used to say which thing, place, idea or person would be the best choice.

given sth when you consider sth; because of sth. SYN in view of sth FML.

content the subject matter and ideas in sth such as a course of study, programme, etc.

as far as sth is concerned used for saying which person or thing you are talking about.

your best bet INF used to tell sb what is the best action for them to take.

put sb up let sb stay at your home.

tied up very busy.

get together meet socially.

thrilled very pleased and excited.

Different jobs

These are all **classed as skilled ▼ manual** workers: **carpenter**, **plumber**, **electrician** and **bricklayer**.

bricklayer

These jobs might be classed as either **semi-skilled ▼** or **unskilled ▼**, with no **qualifications** usually required: **labourer**, **dustman**, and postman.

dustman

These people often work in the **high street**: **florist**, **travel agent**, **estate agent**, **cashier**, **pharmacist**, **librarian**, **traffic warden**. They may work outdoors, or in a shop, or at a desk or **counter.**

WORD FOCUS

A **skilled** job is one that requires a lot of training and experience. A **semi-skilled** job requires some training or experience. An **unskilled** job requires no special training or experience.

---

class sb/sth as sth decide that sb/sth is a particular type of person or thing. SYN **classify sb/sth** v.

manual involving the use of your hands.

carpenter sb who makes things using wood.

plumber sb who fits or repairs such things as water pipes, toilets, etc.

electrician sb who fits or repairs electrical equipment.

qualifications sth such as a degree or diploma that you get when you successfully finish a course of study.

labourer sb who does unskilled physical work, especially outside.

high street the main commercial street in a town with a lot of shops and businesses in it.

florist sb who arranges and sells flowers; the shop is also called a **florist('s)**.

travel agent sb who arranges travel for people. The business is a **travel agency**.

estate agent sb who helps people to rent, buy and sell flats and houses.

cashier sb whose job is to give or receive money in a shop, bank, etc.

pharmacist sb who prepares medicines for sale in a **pharmacy** or **chemist('s)**.

librarian sb who works in a **library** (= a place where you can borrow books).

traffic warden sb whose job is to check that cars and other vehicles are parked legally.

counter a long, flat surface where customers are served in a shop, bar, etc.

23.2 Jobs and duties

I'm a **civil servant**, working for the Department of Trade and Industry. I'm **head** of my section.

I'm an **administrator**. I help to **run** a local community centre.

I'm the **managing director** of a large company.

I'm a **human resources** manager. We **recruit** and **train** over 300 people.

I'm a clothes **designer** ▼ and I **specialize in designing** children's clothes for a large department store.

I'm a food **importer**. I **import** tea from different parts of India and China.

I'm a **priest**. My church is in Paris.

I'm a factory **supervisor**, and I make sure that our products are **up to standard**.

I'm a **social worker**. I often work with children from **deprived** backgrounds.

WORD FOCUS

A **designer** is someone who plans and draws how something will be made: *a fashion/jewellery/software designer*. **design sth** v.

civil servant sb who works for the
civil service (= all government
departments).

head the person in charge of a group.

administrator sb whose job is to manage
and organize an office or institution.

run sth organize or control sth.

managing director the person with the
most senior position in a company.

human resources the department in a
company that deals with employing and
training people. SYN personnel.

recruit sb find new people to join
a company or organization.
recruitment N.

train sb teach sb how to do sth, usually a
skill for a job. training N.

specialize in sth become an expert in a
particular area of work or study.

importer a person or company that buys
goods in another country to sell them
in their own country. import sth V. OPP
exporter N, export sth V.

priest sb who is qualified to perform
religious duties and ceremonies in the
Christian Church.

supervisor sb who is in charge of an
activity or group of workers, and makes
sure things are done correctly.

up to standard at the required level.

social worker sb who is trained to help
people with serious social problems.

deprived not having the things that are
necessary for a comfortable life.

Job prospects

And now a report from our Economics Correspondent, Andrew Turner:

'With the economy still quite **fragile**, **job prospects** are not looking good. The government has said it is expecting some progress in **the private sector**, but unfortunately, **the public sector** could **suffer** more job **losses** with the series of **cutbacks** that have been announced recently. The **construction** industry is also **struggling**, which is bad news for **developers** and, of course, the many jobs that depend on a **prosperous** building industry. But the worst news of all could be for the unemployed who are now in their fifties. It is feared that those **out of work** for over a year may never work again, so **retirement** could come much sooner than they **anticipate**. Elsewhere in the economy, **GPs** and hospital doctors continue to earn high salaries, and the **recovery** in the **banking sector** is continuing.'

fragile not strong or healthy.

prospects PL N the chances of being successful: *job/career prospects*.

the private sector the part of a country's economy that is not under the direct control of the government. OPP the public sector.

suffer sth experience sth bad.

loss the process of losing sth.

cutback a reduction in sth such as the amount of money that is available to spend. **cut sth back** v.

construction the activity of building sth; the industry of putting up buildings.

struggle try to do sth that is very difficult.

developer a person or company that buys land or buildings in order to build new houses or improve old ones.

prosperous rich and successful. **prosper** v.

out of work without a job. SYN unemployed.

retirement the period of time after people stop working (often at 60 or 65). **retire** v.

anticipate sth think that sth will probably happen.

GP (ABBREV General Practitioner) a doctor trained in general medicine, working in the community, not in a hospital.

recovery the process of improving or becoming stronger again. **recover** v.

sector a part of an area of activity, especially of a country's economy: *the banking/financial/manufacturing sector*.

23.4 Job satisfaction

According to Hackman and Oldham (1976), how **satisfying** a job is can be **measured** according to these five **criteria**:

- Skill **variety**: A **challenging** ▼ job using **varied** skills is likely to be more satisfying that a routine, **predictable** job.

- **Task** identity: People who complete a task are likely to be more satisfied than those who only **undertake** a part of it.

- Task **significance**: Jobs are more satisfying if workers feel the task is making a **contribution** to the organization or larger community.

- **Autonomy**: Being able to **use** your **initiative** and make decisions is more satisfying than being told what to do.

- **Feedback**: It is important to get feedback on what you do. Positive feedback makes people feel that they are **valued** and their work is **meaningful**.

WORD FOCUS

If a job is **challenging**, it is difficult in an interesting way and tests your ability. SYN **demanding**. People who want to change their job often say they are looking for a **fresh/new challenge**.

---

satisfying making you feel pleased or happy. **satisfaction** N.

measure sth OFTEN PASSIVE decide how good or bad sth is.

criterion (PL **criteria**) a standard or principle by which sth is judged.

variety the quality of not being the same all the time. **varied** ADJ.

predictable if a job is predictable, you know in advance what will happen, or what you will have to do. OPP **unpredictable**.

task a piece of work that has to be done, especially a hard or unpleasant one.

undertake sth FML agree to be responsible for a job or project and start doing it.

significance the importance of sth, especially when it has an effect on what happens in the future. **significant** ADJ.

contribution sth that you do that helps to achieve sth and make it successful.

autonomy the ability to act and make decisions without being controlled by anyone else. **autonomous** ADJ.

initiative the ability to act on your own without waiting for sb to tell you what to do: *use your initiative.*

feedback advice, criticism or information about how good or useful sb's work is.

valued if you are valued, other people think that what you do is important.

meaningful serious and important.

23.5

Industrial disputes

Airline dispute continues

The long-running **dispute** at Acorn
Airlines shows no sign of being **resolved**.
The **unrest**, which began last year when
the airline **made** a number of workers
redundant ▼, has now **escalated** with
the company's decision to introduce
a two-year **pay freeze**. Company boss
James Critchley believes the action is
necessary to **safeguard** existing jobs
and help them in their attempt to
restructure the business. The **union**,
however, takes a different view, and
has decided to **ballot** its members on
a possible **strike**. They say they are still
prepared to sit down for **talks** in an
attempt to **negotiate** a deal, but it seems
unlikely that they will be able to reach
a **settlement** unless both sides show
more willingness to **compromise**. The
airline said last night that they would
continue to act in the best interests of
the company, but it is difficult to see how
this might **break the deadlock**. •

WORD FOCUS

If somebody **is made redundant,** they
are told they must leave their job
because they are no longer needed.
SYN **be laid off. redundancy** N.

dispute a disagreement between two people, groups or countries.

resolve sth FML find a solution to sth.

unrest a situation in which people are angry and likely to fight or protest.

escalate become worse or more serious. escalation N.

pay freeze the act of keeping pay at a particular level for a period of time.

safeguard sth/sb protect sth/sb from harm or damage.

(trade) union an organization of workers in a particular industry that exists to protect their interests, improve conditions, etc.

ballot sb ask sb to vote in writing and secretly about sth. (secret) ballot N.

strike a time when workers refuse to work because of a disagreement over pay or conditions: *go on strike*.

talks PL N discussions between people from opposite sides to try to reach an agreement.

negotiate sth try to reach an agreement about sth by discussing it in a formal way.

settlement a formal agreement that ends a disagreement.

compromise solve a problem by accepting that you cannot have everything you want. compromise N: *reach a compromise*.

deadlock a situation in which neither side in a disagreement is prepared to change their opinion: *break the deadlock*.

23.6 Apprenticeships

Companies can **benefit** a great deal **from taking on apprentices** ▼.

- As apprentices are given the correct **tools** to do a job and are carefully **monitored**, the quality of their work is often better than that of non-apprentices.

- Businesses with apprentices often find that costs are lower because of improved **productivity**, government **funding**, and a lower wage bill. (Apprentices accept low wages **in return for** the high standard of training they receive.)

- Apprentices are **motivated** and so employee satisfaction tends to be higher. **Apprenticeships** ▼ also provide the **foundation** for later management **roles** and **career** progression.

- Staff **retention** is higher because apprentices are more likely to **stick with** the company than non-apprentices.

- Businesses which offer apprenticeships find it easier to **recruit** able people.

WORD FOCUS

An **apprentice** is a young person who works for an employer for a fixed period of time in order to learn particular skills needed in a job: *an apprentice chef/electrician*, etc. This period of time is an **apprenticeship**.

benefit from sth do well or improve because of sth.

take sb on employ sb.

tool a thing that helps you to make or do sth, e.g. hammer, drill.

monitor sb watch sb carefully over a period of time to see how they develop.

productivity the rate at which goods are produced, especially in relation to the time, money and number of workers needed to produce them. **productive** ADJ.

funding money given for a particular purpose by the government or an organization.

in return (for sth) as a way of thanking sb or paying them for sth they have done.

motivated enthusiastic and determined to do well. **motivation** N.

foundation an important early part of sth from which the rest grows and develops.

role the function or position that sb has in an organization, in society, or in a relationship.

career the series of jobs that you do in your working life, often with increasing responsibility.

retention FML the continued use or possession of sth. **retain sth/sb** v.

stick with sth INF continue with sth or continue doing sth.

recruit sb (to do sth) find new people to join a company or organization.

Company growth

Companies often **point to** external factors to explain their **downfall**: falling demand, cheap foreign imports, etc. However, research in America suggests that **operational** improvements within a company can **account for** 60% or more of its future **potential growth**, and it gives *Metro* as a perfect example.

Metro is Canada's third largest food **retailer** ▼. It has been **targeted** by **giant** American stores such as *Walmart* and *Costco*, but has continued to **flourish** as a result of its operational excellence:

- **emphasizing** high-quality fresh foods where others can't **compete**.

- continually **evaluating** and **adjusting** store locations to account for changing **demographics** and consumer behaviour.

- reducing its **distribution** costs.

- making senior **executives** *live* the business. As one executive explains, "on a wet weekend, the **CEO** will take senior executives to check out the price of peas at **competitors**' stores."

WORD FOCUS

A **retailer** sells goods directly to the public. A **wholesaler** sells goods to shops and small businesses, i.e. retailers.

point to sth mention sth because you
    think it is important.
downfall a loss of success, power, etc.
operational relating to the way that a
    system or business works.
account for sth explain the reason for sth.
potential able to develop into sth in
    the future.
growth an increase in the number, size or
    importance of sth.
target sth select sth for attention or (in
    business) for takeover.
giant extremely large. giant N.
flourish be very successful.
emphasize sth give particular attention or
    importance to sth. emphasis (on sth) N.
compete (with sb) try to be more
    successful than other people or
    companies. competition N.
evaluate sth think carefully about the
    quality or value of sth. SYN assess sth.
adjust sth change sth slightly in order
    to make it better, more effective, etc.
    adjustment N.
demographics the particular features of a
    population such as age, race, etc.
distribution the process of supplying
    goods to shops from one central place.
executive a senior manager in a business.
CEO (ABBREV Chief Executive Officer)
    the most senior manager in a business.
competitor a company that sells the
    same goods or services as your
    own company.

24.2

How to sell

The art of selling

To be successful in selling you need to be both **optimistic** and **persistent** ▼, otherwise your efforts will be **sporadic** and **half-hearted**. At the same time though, you mustn't **get carried away**; be realistic. If you have any serious **reservations** about a sales **campaign**, don't **launch** it before getting feedback from others; this is **crucial**. If you've **invested** a lot of time and thought **in** a campaign, you may not be able to **step back** and be **objective** about it.

You also need to **get into the habit of** thinking like a customer. What makes you **loyal** to a particular company or product, and what **puts you off**?

Try **shifting** your **focus**. Don't concentrate your message on **features** of the product itself – what it is made of or what it looks like – but how the product will actually help and benefit the customer.

WORD FOCUS

If you are **persistent**, you are determined to do something, even though it is difficult. If you are **pushy** (INF and DISAPPROVING), you try hard to get what you want, especially in a way that seems rude.

optimistic feeling that good things will happen. optimism N.

sporadic happening only occasionally.

half-hearted without enthusiasm or effort.

get carried away (by/with sth) get very excited or lose control of your feelings.

reservation OFTEN PL a feeling of doubt about a plan or idea. SYN misgiving(s).

campaign a series of planned activities that are intended to achieve a commercial or political goal. You launch (= start) a campaign.

crucial extremely important for the success of sth.

invest sth (in sth) spend time and effort on sth that you think is good or useful.

step back think about a situation calmly as if you are not involved in it.

objective not influenced by personal feelings or opinions. OPP subjective.

get into the habit of doing sth start doing sth regularly.

loyal willing to support sb, even in difficult times. loyalty N.

put sb off make sb dislike sth.

shift sth move sth from one place or position to another.

focus 1 careful concentration on sth (see text). 2 the thing that you are concentrating on. focus (on sth) v.

feature an important or typical aspect of sth.

24.3 Firms in crisis

Pharma companies in crisis

The **pharmaceutical** industry will move away from **in-house innovation** and move towards greater **diversification**. This **prediction** follows a **survey carried out** by German **analysts** Roland Berger, who found that 65% of companies believe the industry is facing a '**strategic crisis**', with diversification the most common **ploy** to **avert** it.

They **conducted** the survey across 25 companies, including seven of the top ten global firms. The main problem they found was that more than half of the industry's sales rely on **patents** ▼ that will **expire** over the next three years. Many companies will, therefore, lose the advantage that patents bring them, and they could decide to focus less on expensive **innovative** medicines, and instead **diversify** into more **generic** products. •

WORD FOCUS

A **patent** is an official document that gives an **inventor** the legal right to make or sell their **invention** for a period of time, and prevents somebody else from doing so. **patent sth** v.

pharmaceutical relating to the production, use or sale of medicines and drugs.

in-house done or happening inside a company: *in-house training*.

innovation the introduction of new ideas or ways of doing sth. innovative ADJ.

diversification the development of a wider range of products, activities, etc. in order to be more successful. diversify V.

prediction a statement that says what you think will happen. predict sth V.

survey a study of the opinions or experience of a large group of people, based on a set of questions.

carry sth out do and complete a task, survey, enquiry, etc. SYN conduct sth V.

analyst sb whose job involves examining facts or materials in order to give other people information about them. analysis N. analyse sth V.

strategic relating to or forming part of an overall plan to achieve sth. strategy N.

crisis a time of great difficulty or danger.

ploy an action that is carefully planned in order to gain an advantage over others.

avert sth stop sth bad or dangerous from happening.

expire if an agreement or document expires, the period of time it exists for comes to an end. SYN run out.

generic (of a product, especially a drug) not using the name of the company that made it.

The stock market

The stock market value of a **share** is
what an **investor** ▼ is willing to pay for
it. That is **determined** by a **combination**
of factors: the likely future success of
the individual company, the **current
economic climate**, political decisions,
etc. **Momentum** can **play a** big **part** too.
Rising prices can often **tempt** buyers
into the market and **trigger** a **surge**
in buying. This **upward** pressure is
further **fuelled** by **speculators** ▼ who
buy shares on a **short-term** basis, **in the
expectation that** they will be able to sell
them later at even higher prices. This
continuous rise in prices is known as
a *bull market*. If prices then start to fall
– for whatever reason – investors may
rush to sell their shares, so contributing
to the **downward** momentum. This
is called a *bear market*, and when this
happens, millions can be **wiped off** the
value of shares in days, if not hours.

WORD FOCUS

An **investor** is a person who buys
shares or property in the hope of
making a future profit. **investment** N.
A **speculator** is a person who does this
in order to make a quick profit; they do
not invest long term.

the stock market the business of buying and selling shares in companies and the place where it happens.

share any of the units of equal value into which a company's value is divided and which are sold to the public in order to raise money.

determine sth calculate and decide sth.

combination the joining together of two or more things.

current happening now, of the present time.

climate a general attitude or feeling: *the current economic/political climate.*

momentum progress or movement that is becoming faster or stronger.

play a part (in sth) be involved in a situation or activity and influence its development.

tempt sb (into sth) attract sb or make sb want to do sth.

trigger sth make sth happen suddenly.

surge a sudden increase in the amount or number of sth.

upward increasing in amount or price. OPP downward.

fuel sth increase sth or make it stronger.

short-term lasting only a short period of time. OPP long-term.

in the expectation (that) = thinking and believing that sth will happen.

wipe sth off (sth) OFTEN PASSIVE remove sth from sth, suddenly and with speed.

24.5

Economic recession

In the early years of the 21st century, **reckless** lending by banks and other financial institutions was a **major** factor in creating the financial crisis of 2007/8, which was then followed by economic **recession** in many countries. There was a **sharp drop** in international trade, industrial **output** fell, unemployment began to rise, and there was a **slump** in **commodity** prices. To make matters worse, **inflation** ▼ started to grow as food and energy prices **soared**. In normal **circumstances**, governments might be expected to increase **interest rates** to **combat** inflation, but in a recession they were forced to cut interest rates in order to help businesses and ordinary house buyers. By 2009, governments had to **step in** and save certain banks which were **on the brink of collapse**, and many economists were **forecasting** that there would be big cuts in **public services** and employment for years to come.

WORD FOCUS

Inflation is the rate at which prices increase, usually expressed as a **percentage** (%): *The inflation rate is 2.8%.* We can talk about **high** or **low** inflation.

---

reckless showing a lack of care about
   danger or the results of your actions.

major very large or important. OPP minor.

recession a period when the economy of
   a country is not successful and business
   conditions are bad: *economic recession*.

sharp (of a change) sudden and rapid.

drop a fall or reduction in the amount,
   level, or number of sth.

output the amount of sth that a person, a
   machine or an industry produces.

slump a sudden fall in sales, prices, the
   value of sth, etc. slump v.

commodity (in finance) a product or raw
   material such as coffee, cotton or metals.

soar rise very quickly.

circumstances PL N the conditions or facts
   that affect a situation.

interest rate the cost of borrowing money,
   usually expressed as a percentage of the
   amount borrowed.

combat sth stop sth bad from happening
   or from getting worse.

step in become involved in order to help
   sb in a difficult situation.

on the brink of sth almost in a new and
   dangerous or exciting situation: *on the
   brink of war/collapse/victory*.

collapse the sudden failure of a system,
   business, etc.

forecast sth say what will happen in the
   future based on the situation now.

public service a service the government
   pays for such as health and transport.

25.1

Political systems

Capitalism is a **system** in which businesses and industry are controlled and run by private individuals, with little government **interference**, i.e. *a free market*. This produces a society in which some people are **better off** than others. At the other end of the political **spectrum** is *communism*, which is based on the **principle** that everything should be under the control of the **state** and everyone **treated** equally. *Socialism* shares certain principles: **socialists ▼ aim to** create a society in which everyone has equal opportunities, and this requires the government to **regulate** parts of the economy and take it **out of the hands** of individuals. However, there are also **fundamental** differences: socialists do not **reject** all forms of capitalism, and do not try to regulate all areas of society. **Bridging the gap between** socialism and capitalism is *social democracy*, which attempts to **incorporate** a modern **welfare state** within a **broadly-based** capitalist system.

WORD FOCUS

People who believe in the systems above are **socialists, capitalists, communists,** and **social democrats.**

system a method of organizing or doing
    things.

interference the act of getting involved in
    a situation where you are not wanted or
    needed. interfere (in sth) v.

better off in a better situation or having
    more money.

spectrum the whole range of ideas,
    qualities, situations, etc. that are
    possible.

principle a theory, belief, or law that sth is
    based on.

state the government or political
    organization of a country.

treat sb behave in a particular way
    towards sb: *treat sb well/badly*.

aim (to do sth) hope or intend to do sth.

regulate sth control sth using rules.

out of your hands if sth is out of your
    hands, it is not your responsibility.

fundamental of central importance.

reject sth refuse to accept or consider an
    idea, argument, etc. rejection N.

bridge the gap (between A and B)
    reduce or get rid of the difference
    between two groups or things.

incorporate sth add or include sth as part
    of sth else.

(the) welfare state a system by which
    the government provides health care
    and financial help for people who
    need them.

broadly-based based on many kinds of
    things or people.

25.2

Political views

'I'm a socialist **through and through**. I've voted for the same **party** all my life.'

'I used to be quite **left-wing** ▼, but now I would probably **describe myself as** being more or less in **the centre**.'

'I **tend to** be quite **conservative** in most of my beliefs, but not **ultra-**conservative or **reactionary**.'

'I think I'm fairly **liberal** on social **issues**, but perhaps more conservative on economic issues.'

'I've always been fairly **radical**, ever since university.'

'I hate **ideology** – left-wing or **right-wing** ▼ – because people who are **ideological** tend to be quite **dogmatic**.'

'I think I'm probably quite **middle-of-the-road** in most of my views.'

'I would describe myself as **apolitical**, but my brother just says I'm **apathetic**.'

WORD FOCUS

A person who is **left-wing/on the left/a left-winger** believes in socialism (see p.290). A person who is **right-wing/on the right/a right-winger** is more conservative in their political views.

through and through in every way.

party a political organization which you
can vote for in elections: *political party*.

describe sb as sth say that sb is a
particular type of person.

the centre a political position which is
neither left-wing nor right-wing.

tend to do sth often do a particular thing
or be likely to do a particular thing.

conservative supporting right-wing
policies, e.g. a free market and private
ownership.

ultra- PREFIX extreme or extremely.

reactionary DISAPPROVING not wanting
political or social change.

liberal supporting individual freedom and
gradual social and political change.

issue a subject that people discuss or
argue about.

radical wanting major political or social
change.

ideology a set of ideas and values on
which a political or economic theory is
based. ideological ADJ.

dogmatic DISAPPROVING being certain
that your beliefs are right and that
others should accept them.

middle-of-the-road (of people) not
extreme; (of policies) acceptable to
most people. SYN moderate.

apolitical not interested in politics.

apathetic not interested in anything
and not prepared to make an effort
to change.

25.3

Elections

The United Kingdom **general election** ▼ of 2010 was **held** ▼ on 6 May to **elect** ▼ the 650 Members of Parliament who **comprise the House of Commons**. It was a **historic** election, as none of the major parties achieved the 326 **seats** needed for an **overall majority**. This left two **options**: either the Conservatives (the largest party) could attempt to form a **minority government**, or they could try to form a **coalition** with the Liberal Democrats (the third largest party). After five days of **hectic negotiation**, an **agreement** between the **leaders** of the two parties was reached. It meant that both parties had to **abandon** some of their **policies**, and both had to accept policies they had previously fought against during the election **campaign**.

WORD FOCUS

An **election** is an opportunity for people to choose who they want to represent them, usually by **voting** (= showing your choice by making a mark on an official piece of paper). **elect** v. In the UK, **general elections** (to choose the government) **are held** (= take place) at least every five years.

comprise sth be the parts that form sth.

the House of Commons (in Britain) the part of parliament whose members are elected by the people of the country.

historic important in history, or likely to be thought of as important in the future.

seat an official position as a member of a parliament, council, committee, etc.

overall majority (in an election) more votes won than all the other parties added together.

option a choice. **optional** ADJ.

minority government a government that has fewer representatives in parliament than the total number held by all the other parties.

coalition a government formed by two or more parties working together.

hectic very busy and with a lot of activity.

negotiation formal discussion between people who are trying to reach an agreement. **negotiate (sth)** v.

agreement an arrangement or decision about what to do, made by two or more people, groups or organizations.

leader sb who is responsible for a group, organization, country, etc.

abandon sth stop supporting sth such as a policy, an idea, a plan, etc.

policy a set of ideas that a group of people have all agreed on.

campaign a series of planned activities that are intended to achieve a particular aim.

25.4

Party manifesto

These are just a few of the promises that a political party made in a recent election **manifesto ▼**:

- We will **cut red tape** in business practice
- We will **reform** the tax system
- We will **conduct** a **comprehensive review** of defence **spending**
- We will **guarantee** that health spending increases **in real terms**
- We will examine ways to **simplify** the **benefits** system
- We will support the **provision** of nursery care to all pre-school children
- We will introduce **measures** to protect wildlife and we will promote high standards of farm animal **welfare**
- We will **push for** peace in the Middle East
- We will **establish** a new high-speed rail network.

WORD FOCUS

A **manifesto** is a written statement expressing the aims and plans of an organization, especially a political party before an election. It includes the party's **policies** (= a set of ideas that a group of people agree on).

cut sth make sth less in size, amount, etc.

red tape official rules and documents that are unnecessary and cause delays.

reform sth improve a system, organization, etc. by making changes to it.

conduct sth FML organize and do a particular activity: *conduct an experiment*.

comprehensive including many details or aspects of sth. SYNS complete, full.

review an examination of sth, with the intention of changing it if necessary.

spending the money spent on sth, especially by a government or large organization.

guarantee sth promise that sth will happen or promise to do sth.

in real terms after including everything that affects the real value of sth.

simplify sth make sth easier to do or understand. simplification N.

benefits money provided by the government to people who are unemployed, ill, etc.

provision the act of supplying sb with sth that they need or want.

measure an official action that is taken to achieve a particular aim.

welfare the general health and safety of a person, animal or group.

push for sth try to make sth happen because you think it is important.

establish sth make sth start to exist or happen.

25.5

Local politics

Your voice counts!

We asked you to tell us about the issues that **concerned** you here in our town. Here are a few replies from a **cross section** of our readers.

"My main **concern** is the amount of **litter** and **graffiti** everywhere. It's disgusting!"

"For me, the **closure** of the Newgate post office has been a real **blow** to locals, especially **pensioners**, who will now have to go into town for the nearest post office."

"We've got to do something about the **rowdy** and **antisocial behaviour** on our streets late at night; it's terrible!"

"I think **residents** should get **priority** with the **allocation** of parking spaces."

"In my opinion, the new museum building is a **real eyesore**. Who **granted** permission for that?"

"I'm deeply **opposed to** ▼ building another car park in the town centre, when what we **desperately** need to do is encourage more people to use the **park and ride**." •

WORD FOCUS

If you **oppose sth** or **are opposed to sth**, you disagree with it strongly. OPPS **be in favour of sth, support sth**.

concern sb worry sb. concern N.

cross section a group representing a wide
    range of people or things.

litter things such as pieces of paper that
    people leave in a public place, making
    it look untidy. (You should put it in a
    litter bin.)

graffiti PL N drawings or writing on a wall,
    etc. in a public place.

closure the situation when a school,
    factory, etc. shuts permanently.

blow an event that causes you to be sad,
    disappointed, or shocked.

pensioner sb who receives a pension (= a
    regular sum of money you get from the
    government when you reach the age to
    stop working).

rowdy noisy and rather wild.

antisocial behaviour behaviour that shows
    no care for other people or society.

resident sb who lives in a particular place.

priority a right given to you before it is
    given to other people.

allocation the process of dividing sth
    among a number of people.

eyesore a building, object, etc. that is ugly
    and unpleasant to look at: *a real eyesore.*

grant sth allow sb to have sth that
    they want, especially legal or formal
    permission.

desperately with urgency; very much.

park and ride a system in which drivers
    leave their cars in a place outside town
    and travel by train or bus into town.

Newspapers

Why do you read a daily paper?

'I like to follow **current affairs**, and *The Globe* has a high standard of **investigative journalism** ▼. The articles are **detailed** and **unbiased**, which I appreciate.'

'I read *The Sketch* on the way to work; it's **given away** free at the station. It has very good film and TV **reviews**: they're **witty** and entertaining.'

'I like *The Daily Star*. I know it's a bit **downmarket**, but it's **a good read**, and the sports **coverage** is great. I love the **cartoons** too!'

'Actually, I don't read the papers very often. I hate the **tabloids**: they're full of **trivial gossip** about **celebrities**, and they give **the press a bad name**. Some of the stuff they **publish** should be **censored**.'

WORD FOCUS

Journalism is the collecting of news stories for newspapers, TV, etc. This work is done by **journalists** or **reporters**. **Investigative journalism** is the careful and detailed analysis of events in order to discover the truth behind different news, e.g. crime, political corruption.

current affairs political, social and
    economic events that are happening now.

detailed including many small facts.

unbiased fair and not influenced by
    personal opinions. OPP biased.

give sth away give sth to sb without
    asking for any money for it.

review an article giving sb's opinion of a
    play, film, book, etc.

witty funny and clever.

downmarket cheap and of not very good
    quality. OPP upmarket.

a good read sth that is enjoyable to read.

coverage the reporting of news and sport
    in newspapers and on TV and the radio.

cartoon an amusing drawing in a paper,
    especially about politics or current events.

tabloid a newspaper with pictures and
    short articles, less serious than a
    broadsheet (= a newspaper generally
    considered serious).

trivial not important or serious.

gossip informal stories about sb's private life
    that may be unkind or not true. gossip v.

celebrity a famous person.

the press newspapers and magazines.

a good/bad name a good/bad reputation
    (= opinion about sb/sth held by a lot of
    people).

publish sth make information available to
    people in a book, newspaper, etc.

censor sth remove parts of a book, film,
    etc. for moral, political or religious
    reasons. censorship N.

News headlines

Pay curbs for teachers	curb sth that controls or puts limits on sth. curb sth v.
Health service axes top jobs	axe sb/sth remove sb from their job.
Airport hit by strikes	hit sb/sth have a bad effect on sb/sth.
Minister urges fresh talks with unions	urge sth advise or try hard to persuade sb to do sth.
Suspects held in murder probe	hold sb keep sb prisoner.
	probe a full and careful investigation of sth.
Leaders clash in parliament	clash argue or disagree seriously with sb in public.
Two injured in factory blaze	blaze a very large fire, especially a dangerous one.
Mayor vows not to quit	vow to do sth make a serious and formal promise to do sth.
	quit INF leave your job. SYN resign.
Bomb blast injures residents	blast explosion.

Aid spending boost expected — aid food, money, etc. sent to help countries in difficult situations.
boost an increase in sth: *boost in sales.* boost sth v.

Bomb plot foiled — plot secret plan made by a group of people to do sth wrong or illegal.
foil sth stop sth happening, especially sth illegal.

Bid to end flood threat — bid an attempt to do, get or achieve sth. bid v.
threat the possibility of danger, trouble or disaster.

Mid-air drama on transatlantic flight — drama an unusual or exciting event.

WORD FOCUS

Newspaper headlines often consist of short words, e.g. **hit**, **urge**, **bid**, to save space. Some words are used to add a dramatic effect, e.g. **blast**, **drama**, **blaze**, **clash**.

What's on TV tonight?

The Ryder Cup:	**broadcast live** from Chicago, **presented** ▼ **by** Gaby Logan
The Apprentice:	business **reality show**
Seven Days:	a seven-part crime **serial**
Friday Night Live:	**chat show** with famous **guests, hosted** ▼ by Denis Carr
Autumnwatch:	nature **series**. This week: sea eagles on the Isle of Mull
David Copperfield:	popular **costume drama** (a **repeat** of **episode** 4)
Question Time:	**topical debate** in front of a live audience, **chaired** ▼ **by** David Dimbleby
Match of the Day:	**highlights** of Fulham v Manchester City
Space:	science series. Jack Ellis **reports on** asteroids
Countdown:	words and numbers **game show** in which two **contestants** compete against the clock

WORD FOCUS

If somebody **presents** a programme, they introduce the different parts of it. If someone **hosts** a chat show, they introduce and talk to people taking part in it. If someone **chairs** a debate, they present it and are in charge of it.

broadcast (sth) send out a programme on TV, radio or the internet. broadcast N.

live (of a TV programme) broadcast while the event is happening.

reality show a programme based on real people in real situations.

serial a story on TV, the radio, etc. that is broadcast in several different parts.

chat show a programme in which famous people are interviewed and talk informally.

guest a person, often famous, who takes part in a TV chat show.

series a set of programmes on the same subject or with the same characters.

costume drama a programme or film set in the past. (The actors wear clothes of the period.)

repeat a second showing of a programme.

episode a TV or radio programme that is one of a series about a continuing story.

topical connected to sth happening or of interest at the moment.

debate a formal discussion on a subject.

highlight the most interesting or exciting part of sth.

report on sth present a written or spoken account of an event.

game show a programme in which people play games or answer questions to win prizes.

contestant sb who takes part in a game show.

26.4

TV news

TV news has changed enormously in the last **decade**. 24-hour **rolling news** on specialized TV **channels** means that people can find out what is happening **whenever** ▼ they like, or can get **updates** on dramatic events.

In addition, the rise of the internet has meant that **instant** audio and video clips are available which people can hear or see at their office desk. So, when a news story **breaks**, viewers can **follow** the story minute by minute online.

24-hour news **reporting** does have a **downside**, however. It can become very dull and **repetitive**, causing some viewers to **switch off**. There is also a common criticism that **broadcasters** make too much use of **rumour** and **speculation**, either to get the **viewer**'s attention, or simply to fill **air time**.

Whatever the advantages or disadvantages, it seems that 24-hour news is here to stay, and the **rivalry** between different broadcasters for **breaking news** is certainly **intense**.

WORD FOCUS

Whenever has at least two meanings.
1 *Come whenever you like.* = at any time/on any occasion.
2 *Whenever I think of her, I smile.* = every time.

decade a continuous period of ten years.

rolling news continuous news programmes that you can see 24 hours a day.

channel a television station, e.g. BBC 1.

update a report giving the most recent information about sth.

instant immediate.

break (of news) become known: *breaking news.*

follow sth/sb be interested in the progress or development of sth/sb.

reporting the job of producing written reports or broadcasts about news events.

downside the disadvantage or negative aspect of sth. OPP upside.

repetitive saying or doing the same thing many times so that it becomes boring.

switch (sth) off turn sth off, e.g. a TV.

broadcaster a company that sends out TV or radio programmes.

rumour information or a story that people talk about, which may or may not be true.

speculation the act of guessing about causes or effects of sth, without knowing all the facts. speculate about sth v.

viewer sb who watches television.

air time the amount of time given to sth/ sb on the television or radio.

rivalry a situation in which people, teams, etc. compete with each other. (People who are competing with each other are rivals.)

intense very great or extreme.

26.5 Advertising

Advertising ▼ campaigns aim either to **persuade** people to buy products and services, or to **sway public opinion** and **influence** people's behaviour towards **a** particular **course of action**, e.g. having eye tests, or voting for a political party.

In business, a company **sets out to target** a particular type of consumer and persuade them to buy their product. They may **promote** these products through online **commercials ▼**, or use more traditional **approaches** such as **mailshots** and **billboards**. Nevertheless, TV is still recognized as a very effective form of **publicity**. Many **ads ▼** nowadays are of a very high standard, and they often contain **special effects**, **glamorous images** and memorable **slogans**. That doesn't mean, however, that viewers necessarily enjoy them; they are often considered a **nuisance**.

WORD FOCUS

Advertising is the business of making **advertisements** (= a notice, picture or film telling people about a product or service). SYN **ad/advert** INF. A **commercial** is an advert on TV or the radio.

campaign a series of advertisements that try to persuade people to buy sth.

persuade sb to do sth make sb do sth by giving them good reasons to do it.

sway sb cause sb to change what they think or do. SYN influence sb.

public opinion the opinions that most people in society have about an issue.

a course of action a way of behaving in or dealing with a particular situation.

set out to do sth start to do sth with a particular aim.

target sb decide on a group of people that you want to sell to.

promote sth use advertising to say or show that sth is good.

approach a way of doing sth.

mailshot a letter or advertisement sent to many people at the same time.

billboard a large board at the side of a road, used for putting advertisements on.

publicity information that makes people notice a product, person, etc.

special effects clever images or impressions in a film created artificially by technical means.

glamorous attractive, exciting and related to success or wealth. glamour N.

image a picture on a computer or TV screen.

slogan a short phrase that is easy to remember and is used to advertise sth.

nuisance sth that is annoying.

Types of crime

27.1

CRIME	PERSON	VERB
theft	thief	steal
burglary	burglar	burgle
robbery	robber	rob
shoplifting	shoplifter	shoplift
assault	attacker/ assailant FML	attack/ assault
rape	rapist	rape
arson	arsonist	//////////
murder ▼	murderer	murder
manslaughter	//////////	//////////
fraud	fraudster	defraud
kidnapping	kidnapper	kidnap
forgery	forger	forge
bribery	//////////	bribe

WORD FOCUS

Murder is the crime of killing someone deliberately, i.e. you plan or intend to do it. If somebody tries to murder someone but fails, it is **attempted murder**. After a murder, the police will **carry out** (= do) a **murder investigation**. In informal English, the idiom **get away with murder** means do what you want without being stopped or punished: *I get blamed for everything, whereas my sister gets away with murder.*

theft the act of stealing sth from a person or place.

burglary the act of entering a building illegally and stealing sth.

robbery the act of stealing money or goods from a bank, shop, person, etc.

shoplifting the act of stealing goods from a shop by leaving without paying for them.

assault a physical attack on sb.

rape the act of forcing sb to have sex, especially using violence.

arson the act of deliberately setting fire to sth, especially a building.

manslaughter the act of killing sb illegally but not deliberately, e.g. by driving dangerously.

fraud an occasion of cheating or deceiving sb in order to get money or goods illegally.

kidnapping the act of taking someone away illegally and keeping them as a prisoner, especially in order to get money (called a ransom) before returning them.

forgery the act of copying money, documents, etc. in order to cheat people.

bribery the act of offering money or something valuable in order to get sb to help you, especially by doing sth dishonest. It is often used with the word corruption (= dishonest or illegal behaviour, especially by people in authority): *Politicians were accused of bribery and corruption.*

A crime scene

"Last night police received a **tip-off** about a robbery in Bedminster High Street, but when they arrived at **the scene of the crime**, the robbers had **fled**. The **victim**, a man in his seventies, had been in bed and heard nothing. The police have **appealed for** other **witnesses**, and **in the meantime** are continuing their **investigation**.

And in an earlier **incident** in the same area, a man was **arrested** in Leyton after attempting to **hold up** a local post office. A woman outside the post office saw a man behaving **suspiciously** and **alerted** the police. The man was caught while trying to **get away**, and was taken to Bedminster Police Station where he was later **charged with** ▼ attempted robbery."

WORD FOCUS

If you **accuse sb of doing sth**, you say that they have done sth wrong or committed a crime. If the police **charge sb with sth**, they are accusing that person officially of committing a crime: *The police have charged the man with murder.*

tip-off INF a warning or secret information that you give to sb. **tip sb off** v.

the scene of the crime (also **the crime scene**) the place where the crime happens.

flee (PT/PP fled) leave a dangerous situation or place very quickly.

victim sb who has suffered because of a crime.

appeal (to sb) for sth make an urgent request for people to give you help, money, information, etc.

witness a person who sees a crime taking place. **witness sth** v.

in the meantime in the period between two times or events.

investigation the process of trying to find out how sth happened and who was responsible. **investigate sth** v.

incident sth that happens, especially a violent, criminal or dangerous event.

arrest sb if the police arrest sb, they take them to the police station as they believe that they have committed a crime. **arrest** N.

hold sth/sb up take control of and steal from a place or person, often by using a gun or other weapon. **hold-up** N.

suspiciously in a way that makes people think sth illegal is happening.

alert sb tell sb in authority about a possible danger so that they can take action.

get away escape.

27.3 The legal system

In the **legal** system in Great Britain, every **citizen** has the **right** to equal treatment before the law. More serious crimes are **tried** ▼ in open **court** by a **judge** and **jury**; less serious **cases** are tried by **magistrates**.

Fines, **probation** and **imprisonment** may be given for a **guilty** ▼ **verdict**, and if a person is **convicted of** ▼ murder, there is a **mandatory** life **sentence** throughout Britain. Life imprisonment is also a maximum sentence for a number of other serious **offences** such as robbery, rape and manslaughter (see 27.1 p.310). **Capital punishment** was **abolished** in Britain in 1965 for almost all crimes, and in 1998 it was abolished entirely.

WORD FOCUS

In a **trial**, a person is **tried for** a particular crime, e.g. robbery. The court must look at the **evidence** (= information used in court to try to prove sth). If there is **proof** (= information that shows for certain that sth is true) that someone is **guilty**, they will be **convicted of** the crime and punished. If the evidence shows they are **innocent**, they will be **acquitted** (= go free).

legal connected with the law.

citizen a person who has a legal right to live in a country.

right sth that you are legally or morally allowed to do or have.

court the place where a trial happens.

judge the person in a court who decides how a criminal should be punished, or makes legal decisions.

jury a group of members of the public who listen to a case in a court and decide if sb is guilty.

case a question to be decided in court.

magistrate a person who acts as a judge in the lowest courts of law.

fine a sum of money that must be paid for breaking the law. fine sb v.

probation a system that allows sb not to go to prison if they agree to behave well and report to a probation officer.

imprisonment the state of being in prison.

verdict a decision in court stating if sb is guilty of a crime or not.

mandatory required by law.

sentence the punishment given by a court. sentence sb v. *He was sentenced to six years in prison.*

offence an illegal act. SYN crime. A person who commits an offence is an offender.

capital punishment punishment by death.

abolish sth officially end a law, a system, or an institution. abolition N.

27.4

The role of prison

Prison: Have Your Say

Prison should act as a **deterrent**. If it fails, then it's there to **punish** people.

Prison should be a place where we try to **rehabilitate** people who've been **convicted of** a crime. Unfortunately, many **prisoners reoffend** when they're **released**.

No one should **serve** a **life sentence**. How can you rehabilitate a prisoner who knows they will never be released?

If people are a **threat** to society, we have **no option but to** ▼ **lock** them **away**.

Life **behind bars** must be awful. Imagine being locked up in a **cell** for 23 hours a day. That's just **taking the easy option** ▼; it won't help anyone.

Too many innocent people are **remanded in custody** for weeks or months. That's not right.

Prison is about **justice**. If you break the law, you pay the **consequences**.

WORD FOCUS

If you have **no option but to** do something, it is the only choice you can make. If you **take the easy option** (OFTEN DISAPPROVING), you choose something because it is easy, but not always the best thing to do.

deterrent a thing that makes sb less likely to do sth because they know that sth unpleasant will happen if they do. deter sb from doing sth v.

punish sb make sb suffer because they have done sth bad or wrong. punishment N.

rehabilitate sb help sb to have a normal useful life after they have been sick or in prison for a long time. rehabilitation N.

convict sb (of sth) decide and state officially in court that sb is guilty of a crime.

prisoner a person who is kept in prison.

reoffend commit a crime again. (A person who does this is a repeat offender.)

release sb allow sb to leave a place such as prison or hospital.

serve sth spend a period of time in prison.

life sentence a punishment in which sb is sent to prison for the rest of their life.

threat (to sth/sb) a person or thing that may cause trouble or danger (to sth/sb).

lock sb away/up put sb in prison.

behind bars INF in prison.

cell a small room where a prisoner is kept.

be remanded in custody if sb is remanded in custody, they are kept in prison until their trial begins.

justice the treatment of people that is fair and morally right.

consequence (of sth) the result of sth that has happened, and often a bad result.

A crime story

The story so far…

> **Chief Inspector** Mansfield had just one **suspect** with a **motive** for the murder of Tom Stone, and that was Sophie Downs, Stone's former business partner. She was having an **affair** ▼, and Mansfield **suspected** that Stone knew about it and was **blackmailing** her. Downs had no **alibi** for the time of the murder, but although Mansfield had **questioned** her several times, he **had nothing to show for it** so far. The **forensic evidence** had **revealed** very little, and the police still hadn't found the murder **weapon**–thought to be a kitchen knife, as Stone had been **stabbed** in the chest. There had been no sign of a **break-in** at Stone's flat, which also suggested that the **victim** knew his attacker and had **let** them **in**.

WORD FOCUS

An **affair** can be a sexual relationship between two people, especially when one of them is married to sb else (as above). **Affairs** (PL N) can refer to events and activities relating to the government, politics, etc. of a country or region, or to sb's personal life: *She's in charge of foreign affairs. I don't know about his private affairs.*

chief inspector a senior officer in the police force.

suspect a person the police think is guilty of sth, although they do not have proof. suspect sb (of sth/doing sth) v.

motive a reason for doing sth.

blackmail sb demand money from a person by threatening to tell sb else a secret about them. blackmail N.

alibi sb/sth that shows that a person was in another place when a crime was committed.

question sb ask sb questions about sth, especially officially.

have something/nothing to show for sth have achieved something/nothing as a result of what you have done.

forensic connected with the scientific tests the police use when trying to solve a crime.

evidence information that can be used in a court of law to try to prove sth.

reveal sth make sth known.

weapon an object such as a gun or knife that is used for fighting or attacking sb.

stab sb push a sharp, pointed object, especially a knife, into sb, killing or injuring them.

break-in an entry into a building using force, usually to steal sth. break in/into sth v.

victim a person who has suffered or been killed as the result of a crime.

let sb in allow sb to enter a place.

28.1

Informal language

A: Hi, Luis, **how's it going**?

B: Oh, I'm really **fed up**.

A: Why? **What's up**?

B: Well, a **bloke** I work with owes me five hundred **quid**, but now he's telling me he's **broke** and can't pay me back.

A: Oh, **you're joking**. That's awful!

C: Where's Mum and Dad?

D: Um, Dad's just **popped over** to Anne's, and Mum's watching the **telly**.

C: Oh, right. Well, I'm really tired. I think I'll have **a lie-down** before dinner.

D: Well, good luck – the **kids** outside are making **a hell of a** noise!

E: Do you **fancy** going to Mark's **do**?

F: **No way**! You know what **a pain** Mark is.

E: I thought he was a **mate** of yours.

F: He was till he **nicked** my girlfriend.

G: Right, I**'d better be off**.

H: OK, Roz. **Be seeing you** ▼.

G: Yeah, **cheerio** ▼!

WORD FOCUS

There are many informal ways to say goodbye: **Cheerio. Cheers. Bye. Bye-bye. Be seeing you.**

All items listed below are informal.

how's it going? used for asking sb about their progress or their general situation.

fed up unhappy or bored, especially about a situation that has continued for too long.

what's up? = what's the matter?

bloke a man. SYN guy.

(a) quid (one) pound (£1).

broke having no money. SYN skint.

you're joking used to say you are very surprised at sth sb has just said. SYN you're kidding.

pop over/in/round go somewhere quickly, suddenly or for a short time.

telly TV.

a lie-down a short rest, especially on a bed. SYN kip.

kid a child.

a hell of a … used to give emphasis to what you are saying. SYN a heck of a … .

fancy (doing) sth want (to do) sth.

do a party or other social event. SYN get-together.

no way! used to say that there is no possibility that you will do sth. SYN no chance.

a pain an annoying person or situation. SYN a pain in the neck.

mate a friend.

nick sth steal sth. SYN pinch sth.

be off leave. (I'd better be off = I must go.)

28.2

Spoken responses

Have a piece of cake. ~ **Cheers ▼**!

Can I borrow this? ~ Sure, **go ahead**.

Shall we go now? ~ **It's up to you**.

I'm sorry I'm late. ~ **That's all right**.

Thanks for your help. ~ **Not at all**.

Lend me the car, will you? ~ **Get lost!**

Dara's very kind. ~ Oh, **absolutely**.

Is Brigitte still in Paris? ~ **I guess so**.

It's 40 degrees today! ~ **Good heavens!**

Where's Mike? ~ **I haven't a clue**.

How's the job going? ~ **So far, so good**.

I'll get a taxi home. ~ **You'll be lucky**.

Your office is a mess. ~ **So what?**

I need to see your passport. ~ **What for?**

Will you be there? ~ Yeah, **definitely!**

Jamie said you'd been rude to Sam.

~ **That's a load of rubbish!**

I'm going to tell Mum what you said.

~ **Don't you dare!**

WORD FOCUS

Cheers! has different meanings.
Have a chocolate. ~ *Cheers.* = thank
you.
Happy birthday! ~ *Cheers!* said when
you lift a glass before you drink to wish
sb health and happiness.
Bye! ~ *Cheers, see you!* = goodbye.

---

go ahead used to tell sb they are allowed to do sth. SYNS feel free, help yourself.

it's up to you = it's your decision.

that's all right used to reply to sb who says they are sorry about sth, or who thanks you.

not at all used as a polite reply when sb says thank you to you. SYNS don't mention it, you're welcome.

get lost a rude way of refusing to do sth, or telling sb to go away.

absolutely used to emphasize that you agree with sb.

I guess so used to say 'yes', but without being certain. SYN I suppose so.

good heavens used to show that you are surprised or annoyed. SYN good grief.

I haven't a clue = I don't know. SYNS I've no idea, I haven't the faintest (idea).

so far, so good used to say that things have been successful until now.

you'll be lucky used to tell sb that what they want probably will not happen.

so what? used to say that you do not care about sth or think it is important.

what for? used to ask why sb does sth.

definitely used with or instead of 'yes' for emphasis. definitely not = no.

that's a load of rubbish used to emphasize that you think sth is wrong or stupid.

don't you dare! used to tell sb not to do sth, and that you will be very angry if they do it.

28.3

Vague language

Vague language is used when you don't want or need to be precise.

What do you need to buy?
A: Some **stuff** for my hair.
B: Bread, tea, and **things like that**.

How much is the painting worth?
A: $450 **or thereabouts**.
B: **Round about** $500.

How old is Aunty Marie?
A: **Fiftyish** ▼. Yeah, **fifty-something**.
B: **Getting on for** fifty.

Tim's in banking, isn't he?
A: Yes, **something like that**.

What time do you land in Paris?
A: **Shortly before** two.
B: Two, **give or take** a few minutes.

How many are coming to the party?
A: Fifty **plus**, I'd say.
B: Oh, fifty **or so**.

Have we got any bread?
A: Yeah, there's **masses of** it.

Do you think you'll buy the flat?
A: We'll do it **somehow or other**.

WORD FOCUS

The suffix **-ish** is used after certain numbers and adjectives to make them less definite, e.g. **fiftyish** = about fifty; **longish** hair = quite long.

vague not clearly or fully explained.

stuff INF used to talk about substances, objects, etc. when you do not know the name, or the exact name isn't important.

things/stuff like that INF used when you do not want to complete a list.

or thereabouts used to say that a particular number, quantity, etc. is not exact.

round about approximately.

fifty-something a little older/more than fifty. (Also twenty-something, thirty-something, etc.)

(be) getting on for sth (be) nearly a particular age, time or number.

something like that/on those lines/ along those lines used to express sth in a vague way or say that sth is approximate.

shortly before sth a short time before sth. SYN just before sth. OPPS shortly/just after sth.

give or take (a few minutes/a mile, etc.) used to say that the amount you have just mentioned is nearly correct, but not exactly.

plus used after a number or quantity to show that it might be larger.

or so used after an amount of time, money, etc. to show that the amount is not exact.

masses of sth INF a lot of sth. SYNS loads, stacks, tons of sth INF.

somehow (or other) INF in some way, although you do not know how.

28.4

Spoken link words

A: Have you seen Giorgio recently?

B: Yeah, **as a matter of fact**, I saw him briefly in town a couple of weeks ago. And **to be honest**, I nearly didn't recognize him – he's lost a lot of weight and he looked terrible.

A: Yeah, **apparently** he's lost his job – and Claudia's been very ill, remember.

B: Yes, I knew about Claudia, but that's bad news about the job. **Still**, he's very experienced–he'll find more work.

A: Yeah, but **the trouble is**, he's spending all his time looking after Claudia, so he hasn't got much time to look for work.

B: Poor Giorgio. Oh, **by the way**, did you know that Olivia's going to …?

. . . .

C: Did you ask Gavin to help you move?

D: Yeah, he said he was busy–**in other words**, he couldn't be bothered. **Anyway**, it doesn't matter, because Chris has offered to come round and help.

C: Oh, **talking of** Chris, I need someone to decorate the living room.

D: Well, I know he needs the work–**after all**, he's been unemployed for months. **Mind you**, he's very slow!

as a matter of fact used to comment on sth you have just said, usually adding sth you think the other person will be interested in.

to be honest used when saying what you really think. SYN to tell you the truth.

apparently used to say that you have heard that sth is true, but you are not completely certain about it.

still used to say that sth remains true, despite what has just been said. (It often has the same meaning as 'but'.)

the trouble is used when explaining what is difficult about a situation. (Also **the thing is** used to introduce an important fact, problem or reason.)

by the way INF used to introduce a comment or question which is not related to the subject you were talking about before. SYN incidentally.

in other words used to introduce another way of explaining sth, often more simply. SYN that is to say.

anyway used to change the subject of a conversation. SYN anyhow.

talking of sb/sth INF used when you are going to say more about sth/sb that has already been mentioned.

after all used to give a reason for sth, or to explain sth you have just said.

mind you INF used to add sth that makes a difference to what you have just said.

Saying numbers

Numbers	450 = four hundred and fifty.	No 's' in numbers containing *hundred, thousand*, etc. except when no figure is given, e.g. *hundreds of people*.
Travel	BA 285 = BA two eight five.	For flights, say individual numbers.
'0'	PIN no: 0210 oh two one oh	When spelling out numbers with '0', say **oh** or **zero**.
	0°C = zero	For '0' in science, medicine, economics, etc., say **zero**.
	Chelsea 1 Man U 0 = nil	For '0' in team games, say **nil**. In tennis, 40-0 = forty **love**.
	0-60 in 6 seconds = nought	For numbers, ages, etc., say **nought**.
Fractions	½ = a half; ¼ = a quarter; ¾ = three quarters; ⅛ = an eighth.	Link numbers and fractions with **and**: 2½ = **two and a half**. We often use **of** in phrases: *a fifth **of** all children cannot read.*
Decimals	2.45 = two point four five	Say numbers after the **point** (.) as individual numbers, e.g. *two point four five*, NOT *two point forty-five*.
	0.2 = zero/nought point two	

Phone numbers	2392 = Two three nine two.	Say each number separately; NOT **twenty three ninety two**.
	603 0566 = Six oh three, oh five double six.	The number '0' is said as **oh** or **zero**. Always pause between groups of numbers (see comma).
		If two numbers together are the same, use **double**.
Money	50p = fifty pence/fifty p.	For an amount, use either **pence** or **p**. P is more informal.
	£2.80 = two pounds eighty.	NOT **two pounds and eighty**.
	20p (the coin) = a twenty pence/twenty p piece.	Also **a ten/fifty p piece**, but **a one pound coin**.
Years	AD 410 = AD four ten	**AD** = Anno Domini (410 years after the beginning of the Christian calendar; **BC** = before the beginning).
	1962 = nineteen sixty-two	**Hundred** is usually omitted: **nineteen (hundred and) sixty-two**.
	2012 = twenty twelve	Say either **twenty twelve**, or **two thousand and twelve**.

29.1 Negative prefixes

These prefixes can be used before certain adjectives to give the meaning 'not'.

un-

She was **unaware** I was in the room.

We have **unlimited** internet access.

The pain in my arm was **unbearable**.

It was very **uncivilized** behaviour.

He was **unsympathetic** when I explained.

in-

They found the book **incomprehensible**.

I'm afraid your tickets are **invalid**.

He often sounds very **insincere**.

dis-

I was pretty **dissatisfied** with the meal.

It's **dishonest** to pretend that you care.

il-

My handwriting is **illegible**.

Millions of people are still **illiterate**.

im-

Some of their actions were **immoral**.

No one's **immortal**, but Ian thinks he is.

ir-

What he said was completely **irrelevant**.

The doctor's behaviour was **irrational**.

unaware not realizing that sth exists or is
  happening.

unlimited not restricted or controlled in
  time, number or amount.

unbearable (of pain or a feeling) so
  extreme that you cannot deal with it.

uncivilized (of behaviour) rude or offensive.

unsympathetic not showing any kindness
  or interest in other people's problems.

incomprehensible impossible to
  understand.

invalid (of tickets, contracts, etc.) not
  legally effective or acceptable.

insincere saying or doing sth that you do
  not really mean or believe.

dissatisfied annoyed because sth is not
  as good as you expected it to be. (A
  person is dissatisfied because sth is
  unsatisfactory.)

dishonest not honest, truthful or sincere.

illegible difficult or impossible to read.

illiterate not able to read or write.

immoral (of people and their behaviour)
  not considered to be good or honest.

immortal living or existing forever.

irrelevant not important or not connected
  to what you are discussing or doing.

irrational done or happening without clear
  or sensible reasons.

WORD FOCUS

Removing the prefixes gives all of these
adjectives the opposite meaning, e.g.
mortal/immortal, relevant/irrelevant.

29.2 Prefix un-

Un- is the most commonly used prefix for giving adjectives a negative meaning, e.g. *unhappy, unkind, unfriendly, unable.*

'It was **uncharacteristic** of Sam to be so **uncooperative** – he's usually helpful.'

'I'm **unfamiliar with** his books.'

'Amy's parents seemed **unconcerned** that she stayed out late.'

'Alan is rather **unconventional**, so his behaviour can be **unpredictable**.'

'It's **unfortunate** that the TV coverage of the election has been so **unbalanced**.'

'As a boss, he's **unscrupulous**, which explains why he's so **unpopular**.'

'We get **unrestricted** access to the computers at school, which is great.'

'I think we are fairly **unrepresentative** of a typical family.'

'I find the children very **unresponsive**; perhaps I'm doing something wrong.'

'The girls were wearing completely **unsuitable** clothing for this weather.'

'Peter said the accident was **unavoidable**, but the extent of the damage was still **unexpected**.'

uncharacteristic not typical of sb's usual behaviour, and therefore surprising.

uncooperative not willing to help or work with another person or group.

unfamiliar with sth having no knowledge or experience of sth.

unconcerned not worried.

unconventional different from what most people consider to be usual or normal.

unpredictable changing often, in a way that is impossible to prepare for.

unfortunate if sth is unfortunate, you wish it had not happened or had been different.

unbalanced giving only one view or opinion of a situation.

unscrupulous not honest or fair; without moral principles.

unpopular disliked by many people.

unrestricted not controlled or limited in any way.

unrepresentative not typical of other people or things in the same group.

unresponsive not reacting in a suitable way to sth that sb says or does.

unsuitable not correct or appropriate for a particular situation, purpose or person. SYN inappropriate.

unavoidable impossible to stop from happening.

unexpected surprising because you did not think it would happen.

29.3

Verb prefixes

Some prefixes are used before verbs to give them a particular meaning: the prefix *un-* often 'reverses the action' of a verb. So, in the morning you get up and **get dressed**; at night, you **get undressed** and get into bed. You can also **unlock** a door, **unpack** a suitcase, **undo** a jacket, **unwrap** a present, **untie** a person, etc.

"I'LL UNTIE YOU IF YOU GIVE ME YOUR POCKET MONEY."

Dis- can also reverse the action of the verb, e.g. disappear, **disconnect**.

Mis- often means 'wrongly', e.g. **mislead**, **mishear**, **misinform**.

Re- usually means 'again', e.g. rewrite an essay, rebuild a wall, redo a piece of work, retake an exam, **regain** control.

WORD FOCUS

The prefix *dis-* is also used before verbs to give a negative meaning, e.g. dislike (= not like), disagree, **distrust**, **disallow** and **disapprove**.

---

get dressed put your clothes on. OPP
get undressed.

unlock sth open a door/suitcase etc. using
a key. OPP lock sth.

unpack sth take things out of a suitcase,
box, etc. OPP pack sth.

undo sth open or loosen sth so that it is
not closed or fastened: *undo a belt/coat*,
etc. OPP do sth up.

unwrap sth remove the paper or plastic
from around sth such as a parcel or
present. OPP wrap sth up.

disconnect sth break a link between two
things, e.g. the supply of power to a
machine. OPP connect sth.

mislead sb make sb believe sth that is
incorrect or not true. misleading ADJ.

mishear sth hear sth wrongly.

misinform sb OFTEN PASSIVE give sb false
or incorrect information.

regain sth get sth again that you lost,
especially an ability or land: *regain your
confidence, regain control of an area*.

distrust sb not feel confident that sb is
good, honest, etc. OPP trust sb.

disallow sth say officially that sth cannot
be accepted because it is illegal or not
allowed by the rules. OPP allow sth.

disapprove of sb/sth not have a positive
feeling about sb/sth that you think
is not good or suitable. OPP approve
of sb/sth.

29.4

Over- and under-

Over-, with the meaning 'too much', is used with verbs, nouns and adjectives.

'The shop assistant **overcharged** me.'

'Don't **overcook** the rice.'

'My cousin's been **overdoing it** lately; she needs to take it easy.'

'The comment wasn't meant as a criticism, but she **overreacted**.'

'Mike had a late night and **overslept**.'

'I think his films are **overrated**.'

'Don't **overemphasize** the problem.'

'One of the men took an **overdose**.'

'Gemma is **overqualified** for this job.'

Under-, with the meaning 'not enough', is used mainly with verbs and adjectives.

'Never **underestimate** the opposition.'

'I think nurses are **underpaid**.'

'There are still too many **underprivileged** children in our society.'

'The club facilities are **underused**.'

'We're **understaffed** in our office.'

overcharge sb (for sth) make sb pay too much for sth. OPP undercharge sb.

overcook sth cook food for too long. OPP undercook sth.

overdo it/things work/study, etc. too hard or for too long.

overreact (to sth) respond to sth too strongly, especially to sth unpleasant.

oversleep sleep for too long.

overrate sth OFTEN PASSIVE have too high an opinion of sth. OPP underrate sth.

overemphasize sth treat sth as more important than it really is. overemphasis N.

overdose a dangerously high amount of a drug. overdose (on sth) v.

overqualified having more experience or training than is necessary to do a particular job. OPP underqualified.

underestimate sb think that sb has less power or ability than they really have. If you underestimate sth, you think that sth is smaller, less important, etc. than it really is. OPP overestimate sb/sth.

underpaid not earning enough money for work that you do. OPP overpaid.

underprivileged having less money and fewer opportunities than most people in society.

underused not used as much as it could or should be. OPP overused.

understaffed not having enough people to do the work required. OPP overstaffed.

Noun suffixes

A **suffix** is a letter or group of letters added to a word to form another word. These suffixes usually change adjectives into nouns, e.g. **willing** ADJ, **willingness** N.

-ness	He showed no willingness to help.	the state of being happy and prepared to do sth.
	I couldn't see in the darkness.	the state of being dark, without any light.
	The pain was so bad I lost consciousness.	the state of being awake and able to hear, see and think.
-ity	I believe in equality between men and women.	the state of being equal, especially in having the same rights and opportunities. OPP inequality.
	You need sensitivity to do this job.	the quality of understanding how people feel.
	Weapons are a threat to humanity.	all the people (= humans) who are living in the world.
	Morality is a big theme in the book.	the principles of right or wrong behaviour.
	Visibility is very bad at night.	the state of being able to see or be seen.

These **suffixes** usually change verbs into nouns, e.g. **announce** v, **announcement** N.

-ment	They're hoping to make an announcement soon.	a spoken or written statement that gives information about sth.
	He gave me encouragement.	words or actions that give sb confidence and support.
-ion	She showed her appreciation.	an active feeling of pleasure or thanks when you realize that sth/sb is good.
	We want everyone's participation.	the process of taking part and being active in sth.
	This task requires concentration.	the ability to give all your attention to sth.
-ation	He gave us all inspiration.	a feeling of enthusiasm that helps sb to create or do sth.
	The installation is quite expensive.	the act of putting new systems or equipment in place.
-al	Our plans still need their approval.	official agreement or permission to do sth.
	They gave us a firm refusal.	the act of saying 'no' to sth; refusing to do sth.
-ance	We're waiting for their acceptance.	agreement to a plan, offer, or invitation.

Adjective suffixes

These **suffixes** change nouns or verbs into adjectives, e.g. **accident** N, **accidental** ADJ.

-al
I'm sure the fire was accidental.
My boss can be very critical.
The factory will create additional jobs.

happening without being planned or intended.
saying that you think sb or sth is wrong or bad.
extra; more than first planned.

-able
Our prices are comparable with others.
It's a very desirable place to live.

similar in size, amount or quality to sth/sb else.
FML sth that is desirable has qualities that make you
want it. OPP undesirable.

-ive
Some medicine can become addictive.

My son is not very communicative.
I found the book very repetitive.
The doctor's comments were offensive.

If a drug is addictive, people want to take it more
and more and cannot stop. addiction N.
willing to tell things to other people.
Saying or doing the same thing again and again.
unpleasant and likely to make people upset.

-y	The room was filthy.	very dirty.
	We've got a really messy garden.	untidy and/or dirty.
-ous	Her actions were very courageous.	very brave and determined.
	It was a spontaneous response.	happening naturally, and without being planned.
-ful	Martin said it without thinking; he should've been more tactful.	careful not to do or say anything that could upset someone. OPP tactless.
	It's doubtful he'll come now.	not likely to happen or be true. SYN unlikely.
	She's a very skilful politician.	good at doing sth that involves ability or training.
	My brother is usually very thoughtful; it's one reason why people like him.	showing that you care about others. OPPS thoughtless, inconsiderate. SYN considerate.
-less	It's pointless waiting here any longer.	without any purpose and not worth doing.
	That dog is completely harmless.	unlikely to cause injury or damage. OPP harmful.
	There are endless ways of making money.	seeming to have no end or limit.

341

30.1

Verb + noun 1

Certain verbs and nouns are frequently used together. **Keep a record of** these common word partners.

'I **gave it a try** for a year, but **came to the conclusion** that it wasn't the right job for me, so I **handed in my notice**.'

'The two sides have been **holding talks** for weeks, but they're still no nearer to **breaking the deadlock**.'

'The manager needs to **take action** and **set an example** for the rest of the staff.'

'I tried to **highlight the problem** ▼, but the company **didn't take any notice**.'

'Barry **told** us one of his silly **jokes**, but we still **roared with laughter**.'

'The council has **devised a scheme** that could **bring an end to** illegal parking.'

'Even if they **settle their argument**, I'm not sure it will **make a big difference**.'

WORD FOCUS

Some nouns frequently combine with different verbs:
Can you **solve the problem**?
We need to **tackle the problem**.
I'm sure we'll **overcome the problem**.
(= succeed in dealing with or controlling a problem).

keep a record (of sth) have a written note
of sth that you can use in the future.

give sth a try test sth or make an attempt
to do sth.

come to the/a conclusion make a
decision after thinking about all of the
important information. SYN reach the/a
conclusion.

hand in your notice tell your employer
that you are leaving your job soon.

hold talks (of governments or other
organizations) have formal discussions.

break the deadlock end a situation in
which people have been unable to reach
an agreement.

take action begin to do sth to solve a
problem.

set an example do sth that is considered
a good model for others to follow
and copy.

highlight a problem describe a problem
in a way that makes people notice it.

take notice (of sb/sth) OFTEN NEGATIVE
pay attention to sb/sth.

tell a joke tell sb a funny story.

roar with laughter laugh loudly.

devise a scheme invent a new way of doing
sth. (Also devise a plan/method, etc.)

bring an end to sth stop sth or make sth
stop.

settle an argument end a disagreement.

make a difference have an important
effect on sth, especially a good effect.

30.2
Verb + noun 2

A number of nouns commonly combine with different verbs with opposite meanings. For example, you can **pass an exam** (= be successful in it), or you can **fail an exam** (= be unsuccessful). Here are some more combinations of this type.

You can:

catch or **miss a bus**

obey or **break the law**

keep or **break a promise**

keep or **miss an appointment**

gain or **lose control** (of sth)

accept or **reject an offer**

support or **oppose an idea**

show or **hide your feelings**

adopt or **abandon a policy**

confirm or **deny a rumour**

admit ▼ or **deny** ▼ a crime

impose or **lift sanctions**

WORD FOCUS

If you **admit** a crime or something you have done wrong, you say you have done something illegal or wrong:
He admitted stealing the car.
They admitted the charge of assault.
OPP **deny** a crime:
He denies murder.
She denied taking the bag.

catch a bus get on a bus that is travelling
    somewhere. (If you miss a bus, you are
    too late to get on it: *catch/miss a train/
    plane.*)

obey the law do what a law says that you
    must do. OPP break the law = do sth
    illegal.

keep a promise do sth that you agreed to
    do. (If you break a promise, you fail to
    do it.)

keep an appointment go to a meeting
    that you have arranged. (If you miss an
    appointment, you don't go as arranged.)

gain control (of sth) achieve the power to
    influence a situation. SYN take control
    (of sth). OPP lose control (of sth).

accept an offer say 'yes' to an offer. OPP
    reject an offer.

support an idea agree with an idea and
    want it to succeed. OPP oppose an idea.

show your feelings let people see and
    know how you think or feel about sth.
    OPP hide your feelings.

adopt a policy decide to start following a
    policy. OPP abandon a policy.

confirm a rumour say that a piece of
    information that is being passed around
    about sb/sth is in fact true. (If you deny
    a rumour, you say that the information
    is not true.)

impose sanctions start an official order to
    stop communication, trade, etc. with a
    country that has broken international
    law. OPP lift sanctions.

30.3

Adjective + noun

We had **great difficulty** finding Krista's flat, and it was **pure luck** we got there on time. Still, everyone gave us **a** very **warm welcome** and it was a shame it was such **a brief visit**.

There is now **clear evidence** that the council plans to make **sweeping changes**, with the recent transport cuts being **a perfect example**. Many believe this could have **an adverse effect** on the local economy.

I have **a vivid memory** of staying at my uncle's house as a child. He was **a real character**, though my mum always complained that his place was **a complete mess**.

After strong winds and **torrential rain** caused **widespread damage** over the weekend, forecasters now expect more **severe weather** later this week. Drivers are being urged to take **great care**.

Finding somewhere to live was my **main concern** when I moved to London. Now I've got a flat, a job is my **number one priority**. I've applied for a few and I think I've got **a fair chance** of getting one of them.

great difficulty = a lot of problems.

pure luck luck alone, without the need for effort or ability. SYN sheer luck.

a warm welcome a very friendly way of greeting sb.

a brief visit a short stay at a place.

clear evidence facts or physical signs that are obvious or impossible to doubt.

sweeping changes changes that have a big effect. SYNS major/radical changes.

a perfect example a very good example.

an adverse effect a negative or unpleasant effect. SYN a damaging effect.

a vivid memory a very clear memory.

a real character INF sb with special qualities that makes them different and interesting.

a complete mess a situation in which a place is very untidy or dirty.

torrential rain rain that falls fast in large amounts.

widespread damage damage that exists in many places. SYN extensive damage.

severe weather extremely wet, cold or wild weather. (Also severe pain = very unpleasant pain.)

great care a lot of effort and attention.

(the) main concern the thing causing most worry.

(the) number one priority the most important thing that must be done.

a fair chance a good or reasonable possibility that sth will happen.

30.4 Preposition + noun

Minister **under pressure** to quit

SOLDIERS ACCUSED OF FIRING **AT RANDOM**

PM admits '**in retrospect** I was wrong'

Doctors left patient **in agony**

10% refuse to eat meat **on principle**

Banks **under investigation**

FIRE RAGES **OUT OF CONTROL**

Board will back chairman **within reason**

Firemen to **go on strike at short notice**

Club say manager left **by choice**

Film star refuses to appear **in public**

Union talks take place **behind closed doors**

under pressure if sb is under pressure, there has been an attempt to persuade or force them to do sth.

at random without a particular method, pattern or purpose.

in retrospect thinking now about the past, using knowledge or information that you did not have at the time. SYN with hindsight.

in agony experiencing great pain. (Also in danger/in decline/in trouble.)

on principle because of rules or beliefs that influence your actions.

under investigation in the process of being examined officially to find out the facts of a situation. (Also under discussion/under attack.)

out of control if sth is out of control, you are unable to limit it or make it do what you want. OPP under control.

within reason according to what is practical, possible or sensible.

go on strike refuse to work as a protest about pay or conditions of work.

at short notice without very much warning. SYN at a moment's notice.

by choice because you have chosen sth.

in public when other people, especially people you do not know, are present. OPP in private.

behind closed doors in private; without the public being allowed in.

Adverb + adjective or verb

This information will be vitally important.	extremely important.
I thought the exam was relatively easy.	quite easy. (Also relatively difficult.)
His comments were utterly ridiculous.	extremely silly or stupid. (Also utterly stupid.)
The students were bitterly disappointed with their results.	extremely disappointed, especially showing feelings of sadness or anger. (Also bitterly upset/ashamed.)
My brother's highly unlikely to come.	very unlikely. (Also highly dangerous.)
Most of the children are highly educated.	very well educated. (Also highly paid.)
The bank is directly opposite.	exactly opposite. (Also directly above/below.)
Who's directly responsible for this?	having full and complete responsibility.
The town was virtually empty.	almost empty. (Also virtually full/impossible.)
Both men were fatally injured.	injured so badly that you die. (Also fatally wounded.)
The manager's figures are wildly optimistic.	extremely optimistic. (Also wildly inaccurate.)

Are you quite sure you understand what you have to do?	completely sure. (Also quite right/impossible; I quite understand.)
It's perfectly natural for parents to worry about their children.	completely natural; often used to emphasize a particular quality. (Also perfectly reasonable.)
The meaning is entirely different.	completely different.
When did they arrive? ~ I'm not entirely sure.	not completely sure. (Also not entirely satisfied.)
They're both desperately unhappy at the moment.	extremely unhappy. (Also desperately sad/lonely.)
He desperately wants to win.	= very much wants.
The example clearly illustrates the point.	shows in a way that people can easily see, hear or understand. (Also sb/sth clearly states that ….)
His talents are not fully appreciated.	completely understood or recognized. (Also I fully realize/understand.)

351

Decisions

problem page.org

Should I ask my girlfriend to marry me?

I'm finding it hard to **make up my mind**; I just keep **going round in circles**. My brother's always telling me to **get on with it**, but what worries me is that Jessie and I are still young, and perhaps we should **wait and see** how things **turn out** between us. I don't believe in **rushing into** things.

Should I go and work abroad?

I've been offered a job in the USA, but I keep **putting off** the decision because it's a big move and a risk (I've already got a good job). I could **play it safe** and **stay put**, but then I might **look back** in ten years' time and regret it. Jobs like that don't **come up** very often.

Should I start a business?

I'm in two minds about this. I know it's not a good time to **set up** a business, but at some point in my life, I have to **have the courage of my convictions** and **go for** it. I can always adapt the business **as I go along**, and if I lose money, well, I'll just have to **cross that bridge when I come to it**.

make up your mind decide sth.

go round in circles think or argue about
   sth without making any progress.

get on with it stop wasting time and do
   what you should be doing.

wait and see be patient and delay doing
   sth until you see what happens.

turn out develop in a particular way, or
   have a particular result.

rush into sth do sth without thinking
   carefully about it first.

put sth off arrange to do sth at a later
   date, especially because you do not
   want to do it.

play (it) safe be careful and avoid risks.

stay put INF stay in one place or position.

look back (on sth) think about sth in
   your past. SYN reflect on sth.

come up if a job or an opportunity
   comes up, it becomes available.

be in two minds about sth have difficulty
   in making a decision to do sth.

set sth up start a business, an
   organization, etc.

have the courage of your convictions
   continue to say or do what you think is
   right, even if other people think you are
   wrong.

go for sth INF try to achieve, get or win sth.

as you go along = at the same time as
   continuing with another activity.

cross that bridge when you come to it
   worry about a problem when it actually
   happens and not before.

A good memory?

'I**'ve got a memory like a sieve**. Unless I **jot** things **down** in my diary, I can't remember appointments – especially unpleasant things like going to the dentist. I just **block them out**.'

'I never remember things my mum tells me to do. It just **goes in one ear and out the other** – especially the washing-up.'

'I can't remember people's names. I'm talking to someone, **racking my brains** and hoping their name will **come back to** me. The other day I had to introduce a colleague to someone. Her name was **on the tip of my tongue**, but I just couldn't remember it. So embarrassing.'

'It was June 21st yesterday, which **rang a bell**, but I couldn't think why. Then it suddenly **occurred to** me–my wife's birthday! It was a terrible thing to forget –it just **slipped my mind**. She was furious.'

'I was feeling **stressed out**, and the boss asked me about the sales figures. **My mind went** a complete **blank**. It was my own fault; I should have **made a note of them** before the meeting.'

'I repeat irregular verbs **over and over again**, and eventually they **sink in**.'

have a memory/mind like a sieve INF
have a very bad memory; forget things
easily.

jot sth down write sth quickly. SYNS note
sth down, make a note of sth.

block sth out fail, or decide not to think
about or remember sth unpleasant.

**go in one ear and out (of) the
other** INF be forgotten easily.

rack your brain(s) try very hard to
remember or think about sth.

come back to sb if sth comes back to
you, you remember it or remember
how to do it.

on the tip of your tongue if a word,
name, etc. is on the tip of your
tongue, you know it but you cannot
remember it.

ring a bell INF if sth rings a bell, it
sounds familiar to you, but you cannot
remember exactly what it is.

occur to sb (of an idea or thought)
suddenly come into your mind.

slip your mind if sth slips your mind, you
forget it.

stressed out INF so worried that you
cannot relax. SYN stressed.

go blank if you go blank, or your
mind goes blank, you are unable to
remember sth.

over and over again many times;
repeatedly. SYN again and again.

sink in be understood and remembered.

Time

A: Are the builders **pressing on with** your new kitchen?

B: No, they've **got** a bit **behind with** things, actually. They had to **put back** the electrical work, and now it's **dragging on** longer than expected.

A: Well, I hope things **speed up** a bit.

A: I'm so sorry to **keep you waiting**. Something **cropped up at the last minute**, I'm afraid.

B: That's OK. I'm **not in any hurry**.

A: What time did you **set off**?

B: Early! Sam **turned up at the crack of dawn**, so we left at 6 **on the dot**, and got to the airport **in good time**.

A: Do you ever see Claude?

B: Yes, **from time to time**. Actually, I **ran into** him **the other day** in town.

A: Is Jackie still living with her dad?

B: Yes, **for the time being** at least.

WORD FOCUS

Look up the word **time** in your dictionary for more idioms like these:
Time is money. = time is valuable and must not be wasted.
We **made good time**. = completed the journey quickly.

press on/ahead with sth continue doing sth in a determined way.

get behind with sth if you get behind with work, you have not done as much work as you should have by a particular time.

put sth back change the date or time of an event so that it happens later than planned. OPP bring sth forward.

drag on continue for too long.

speed up move or happen faster.

keep sb waiting make sb continue to wait.

crop up if sth crops up, it happens suddenly or unexpectedly.

(at) the last minute (at) the latest possible time before another event.

not in a/any hurry having plenty of time.

set off begin a journey. SYN set out.

turn up arrive. SYN show up INF.

at the crack of dawn INF very early in the morning.

on the dot at exactly the time mentioned.

in good time early; with enough time so that you are not in a hurry.

from time to time occasionally but not regularly.

run into sb INF meet sb by chance. SYN bump into sb.

the other day/morning/week recently.

for the time being for a short period of time, but not permanently. SYNS for now, for the moment.

Truth and lies

'As a child I used to tell a few **white lies ▼**, but I did it too often, and it **became second nature**. Most of the time I **got away with** it, but I'm sure some people could **see through** my lies.'

'My son **makes up** all sorts of lies to avoid **getting into trouble**. He thinks he can **pull the wool over my eyes**, but he's wrong! Sometimes I don't **let on** that I know he's lying, but later on I ask him a question and **catch him out**. I'm worried, though. It's getting to the stage where I **can't believe a word** he says.'

'My business partner made some bad decisions which affected our profits, but he tried to **cover them up**. For a long time, I was **taken in** by his excuses, but the pressure was too much for him, and he finally **owned up**.'

'I knew she was **keeping** the truth about dad **from** me–the expression on her face **gave the game away**. Maybe she couldn't **bring herself to** say that he was leaving. They'd just **drifted apart**.'

WORD FOCUS

A white lie is a lie you tell sb in order to protect them or avoid hurting their feelings. If you **lie through your teeth**, you say sth completely false.

be/become second nature (to sb) sth
  that is second nature to you is sth that
  you have done so often that you do it
  without thinking.
get away with sth not be caught
  or punished for sth that you have
  done wrong.
see through sth/sb realize the truth
  about sth/sb.
make sth up invent an explanation.
get into trouble be in a situation in which
  you can be punished or criticized.
pull the wool over sb's eyes INF
  try to trick sb by giving them false
  information.
let on (to sb) INF tell sb a secret.
catch sb out make sb make a mistake in
  order to prove that they are lying.
not believe a word used to emphasize
  that you cannot believe what sb says.
cover sth up prevent people from
  discovering a mistake or sth bad.
take sb in OFTEN PASSIVE make sb believe
  sth that is not true. SYN deceive sb.
own up (to sth) admit that you have done
  sth wrong. SYN confess (to sth).
keep sth from sb avoid telling sb about sth.
give the game away let sb know a secret
  or surprise when you did not want or
  intend to let them know.
bring yourself to do sth force yourself to
  do sth that you do not want to do.
drift apart if two or more people drift
  apart, their relationship gradually ends.

Giving advice

If I were you, I'd look for another job.

If I were in your shoes …

… I'd think twice before buying a car from Simon.

I think you'd better ask your wife what she thinks.

You'd be better off staying at school for another year, rather than getting a job.

If you're looking for a flat, your best bet is to look in the local paper.

This phrase is used to give advice; the main clause is **would** + verb.

This phrase also introduces advice and is followed by **would** + verb. SYN if I were in your position.

think carefully before deciding to do sth.

= I think it would be a good idea if you … . **you'd better = had better.**

used to say that sb should do sth else, rather than what they are doing or are planning to do.

SPOKEN used when giving advice to sb.

You could always wait until next year.	used to suggest a possible course of action.
There's no harm in asking for help with your essay.	used to suggest sth to sb. SYNS it would do no harm (to do sth), it wouldn't hurt (to do sth).
You'd be well advised to ask Mr Jackson's permission before you leave early.	used more formally when you are advising sb to do sth which will help them avoid trouble.
It's about time you got a new computer. This one is so slow.	INF used to say that you think sb should do sth soon.
Whatever you do, take your time and don't rush into a decision.	used to warn sb that it is very important to do or not do sth.
If all else fails, you can borrow money from Uncle Erich.	used for saying that if all other methods have been unsuccessful, there is one last thing you can try to do. SYN as a last resort, … .

31.6 Shocks and surprises

'People always said that once you **get the hang of** driving it's easy, but I found it very hard, and I didn't think I **stood a chance ▼ of getting through** my test. But somehow I passed. **I can't believe it**, but I'm absolutely **thrilled to bits**.'

'I thought I was **getting along** quite well at work, so I **was** really **taken aback** when the boss called me in to her office and said I'd have to **pull my socks up** if I wanted to keep the job. It just came **out of the blue**. I still **can't get over it**.'

'Jack's **supposed to** keep his dog **shut in** because it can be dangerous. But when I was in his garden, the dog appeared from nowhere and barked at me. **The next thing I knew**, it was on top of me, but **believe it or not**, it didn't actually bite me; it just wanted to play. Still, it **gave me the fright of my life**.'

WORD FOCUS

There are several idioms with **chance**.
stand a chance (of doing sth) = have the possibility of succeeding in sth.
take a chance (on sth) = decide to do sth, knowing it may be the wrong choice.
the chances are (that) … = it is likely (that) …

get the hang of sth INF learn a skill or
an activity.

get through (sth) be successful in
an exam.

I can't/don't believe it used to emphasize
that you are very surprised or shocked
by sth.

thrilled to bits extremely pleased and
excited. SYN over the moon INF.

get along used to talk about how well
sb is doing in a particular situation.
SYN get on.

be taken aback be shocked or surprised.

pull your socks up INF try to improve
your performance, work, behaviour, etc.

out of the blue INF suddenly and
unexpectedly.

can't get over sth used to say that you
continue to be very surprised or upset
about sth.

be supposed to do sth if you are
supposed to do sth, you should do it
because sb told you to do it, or because
it is your responsibility.

shut sb/sth in put sb/sth in a room or
house and keep them there.

the next thing I knew used to say that a
situation happened very quickly when
you did not expect it.

believe it or not INF used to introduce
information that is surprising but true.

give sb the fright of their life INF make
sb suddenly feel extremely afraid.

Abbreviations

If you want to know the meaning of an abbreviation, use **stand for**:

Q: What does PO **stand for**?
A: (It **stands for**) post office.

Learning English

EFL	English as a foreign language
FCE	First Certificate in English (upper intermediate exam)
CAE	Certificate in Advanced English
CPE	Certificate of Proficiency in English (very advanced exam)
IELTS	International English Language Testing System
EAP	English for Academic Purposes

University qualifications

BA	Bachelor of Arts (first degree)
BSc	Bachelor of Science
MA	Master of Arts (second degree)
MSc	Master of Science
MBA	Master in Business Administration
PhD	Doctor of Philosophy SYN **DPhil** (high level degree involving research)

Organizations

BBC	British Broadcasting Corporation
EU	European Union
UN	United Nations

Business

AGM	annual general meeting
CEO	chief executive officer
HQ	headquarters
HR	human resources (also called *Personnel)*
MD	managing director

Money

ATM	automated teller machine (also called *cashpoint /cash machine)*
PIN	personal identification number (= a number you need, for example, to take money out of a cash machine)
VAT	value added tax (a tax on goods and services in the EU)
APR	annual percentage rate

Medicine

A&E	Accident and Emergency (= a department in a hospital)
AIDS	Acquired Immune Deficiency Disorder
GP	General Practitioner (= a doctor who does not work in a hospital)

WORD FOCUS

Most abbreviations are spoken as individual letters, e.g. E-F-L, but a small number are pronounced as words, e.g. AIDS /eɪdz/, PIN /pɪn/, and VAT /væt/. VAT can also be pronounced as individual letters /ˌviːeɪˈtiː/.

Technology

IT	information technology (= the study or use of electronic equipment)
PC	personal computer
ISP	Internet Service Provider, e.g. AOL
OS	operating system, e.g. Microsoft Windows
CCTV	closed-circuit television (= a TV system in an area, e.g. a building to protect it from crime)
CD	compact disc

People

PM	Prime Minister
MP	Member of Parliament
PA	personal assistant
DJ	disk jockey (= someone who plays CDs and records in a club)
PC	Police Constable
VIP	Very Important Person

Other common abbreviations

B&B	bed and breakfast (= a small hotel that serves breakfast but no other meals)
asap	as soon as possible (also used in in informal written English)
ID	identification
IQ	intelligence quotient (= a measure of a person's intelligence using special tests)

ETA	estimated time of arrival (**ETD** = estimated time of departure)
RIP	rest in peace (used on gravestones after people have died; also **R.I.P.**)
DIY	do-it-yourself

Abbreviations in written English

i.e.	that's to say; in other words (from Latin 'id est')
e.g.	for example (from Latin 'exempli gratia')
etc.	and so on (from Latin 'et cetera')
PTO	please turn over (at the bottom of a page)
FAO	for the attention of (used in formal letters)
PS	postscript (used at the bottom of a letter to add extra information)
NB	take note (= pay special attention to what follows'; from Latin 'nota bene')
RSVP	please reply (from French 'répondez s'il vous plaît')
p.a.	per year (from Latin 'per annum')
encl.	enclosed (also **enc.**)
plc	public limited company

Abbreviations in text messages/emails

IMO	in my opinion
FYI	for your information
LOL	**1** laughing out loud (used to show you think sth is funny). **2** lots of love (used at the end of emails and texts)

British and American English

lorry BrE
truck NAmE

lift BrE
elevator NAmE

rubbish bin BrE
trash can NAmE

bath BrE
bathtub NAmE

tap BrE
faucet NAmE

mobile (phone) BrE
cellphone NAmE

rubber BrE
eraser NAmE

handbag BrE
purse NAmE

wallet BrE
billfold NAmE

sweets BrE
candy NAmE

crisps BrE
potato chips NAmE

chips BrE
(French) fries NAmE

British English	American English	Notes
People		
postman	mailman	
dustman	garbage man	see 23.1
lawyer/solicitor	attorney	see 14.4
mum	mom	
mate INF	buddy INF	a friend.
Transport	**Transportation**	
petrol	gasoline	
petrol station	gas station	see 8.1 (also **service station** in BrE and NAmE)
car	automobile	
roundabout	traffic circle	see 16.1

flyover	overpass	a bridge that carries one road over another road.
overtake a car	pass a car	see 16.1
subway	underpass	a passage that goes underground for people to walk through.
underground/tube	subway	see 16.3
railway	railroad	the system of travelling by train and all the companies, equipment, etc. relating to it.
return ticket	round trip ticket	a ticket for a journey to go and come back again.
pavement	sidewalk	the place at the side of the road where people walk.
zebra crossing	crosswalk	a series of black and white stripes across a road where cars must stop and people can cross the road.
motorway	highway/freeway	a fast, main road used for travelling long distances.

British English	American English	Notes
In town		
block of flats	apartment building	a large building that contains a number of different flats.
terraced house	townhouse	a house that is one in a row of houses which are all joined together.
chemist	drugstore	see 23.1
shopping mall/ shopping centre	mall	see 8.1
shop	store	
off-licence	liquor store	a shop that sells alcoholic drinks in bottles and cans to take away.
car park	parking lot	an area where people can leave their cars.

toilet/loo INF	restroom/john INF	a toilet in a public place or building.
Eating in and out		
biscuit	cookie	a small, sweet flat and dry cake which is usually crisp.
courgette	zucchini	see 12.2
aubergine	eggplant	see 12.2
prawn	shrimp	see 12.4 (A **shrimp** in BrE is a very small prawn.)
grill/barbecue sth	broil sth	cook meat or fish by putting heat above it (= **grill** BrE) or under it (= **barbecue** BrE).
bill	check	a piece of paper that shows how much you must pay for the food and drink you have had in a restaurant. (A **bill** in NAmE is a banknote, e.g. a ten- dollar **bill**.)
café/restaurant	diner	a small restaurant that sells cheap, simple food.

British English	American English	Notes
Clothes		
trousers	pants	
waistcoat	vest	see 13.4
trainers	sneakers	shoes you wear for sport, or as informal clothing.
dressing gown	robe	a long, loose coat that you wear indoors, usually over night clothes.
vest	undershirt	a piece of underwear for the top part of your body.
swimming costume	bathing suit	a piece of clothing worn for swimming, usually by women and girls.
built-in cupboard	closet	a tall cupboard used for storing clothes or things.
jumper/sweater	sweater	

Irregular verbs

This is a selection of irregular verbs, based on verbs and derivatives in Oxford Learner's Pocket Word Skills.

Base form	Past tense	Past participle
awake	awoke	awoken
beat	beat	beaten
become	became	become
bend	bent	bent
bet	bet	bet
bid	bid	bid
bite	bit	bitten
bleed	bled	bled
blow	blew	blown
broadcast	broadcast	broadcast
burn	burnt	burnt
burst	burst	burst
cost	cost	cost
deal	dealt	dealt
draw	drew	drawn
fall	fell	fallen
feel	felt	felt
fit	fitted/fit	fitted/fit
flee	fled	fled
forecast	forecast	forecast
freeze	froze	frozen
grow	grew	grown
hit	hit	hit
hold	held	held
keep	kept	kept

IRREGULAR VERBS

Base form	Past tense	Past participle
lay	laid	laid
lead	led	led
lean	leant/leaned	leant/leaned
leap	leapt/leaped	leapt/leaped
lie	lay	lain [rare]
mean	meant	meant
pay	paid	paid
quit	quit	quit
ride	rode	ridden
ring	rang	rung
rise	rose	risen
seek	sought	sought
shake	shook	shaken
shed	shed	shed
shine	shone	shone
shoot	shot	shot
sink	sank	sunk
speed	sped/speeded	sped/speeded
spell	spelt/spelled	spelt/spelled
spill	spilt/spilled	spilt/spilled
spread	spread	spread
spring	sprang	sprung
stick	stuck	stuck
sting	stung	stung
strike	struck	struck
sweep	swept	swept
swell	swelled	swollen
throw	threw	thrown
tread	trod	trodden
upset	upset	upset
withdraw	withdrew	withdrawn

Quiz answers

10.3 Biology quiz (page 110)

1 T
2 T
3 F
4 T
5 T
6 F (above ground)
7 F (206)
8 F (a mammal, but not marine)
9 T
10 F (before birth)

18.5 Classical music quiz (page 210)

1 Strings
2 Brass
3 Giuseppe Verdi
4 A tenor
5 A soprano
6 Ludwig van Beethoven
7 A conductor
8 For singers
9 A musician
10 At the beginning
11 600
12 Four

Abbreviations used in this book

N	noun
V	verb
ADJ	adjective
OPP	opposite
SYN	synonym
INF	informal
FML	formal
PL N	plural noun
PT	past tense
PP	past participle
BrE	British English
NAmE	North American English
sth	something
sb	somebody
etc.	You use 'etc.' at the end of a list to show there are other things, but you aren't going to say them all.
i.e.	that is
e.g.	for example

Key to symbols

Phonetic symbols

iː	tea	ʊ	book	əʊ	so
ɪ	sit	uː	fool	aʊ	now
i	happy	u	actual	ɔɪ	boy
e	ten	ʌ	cup	ɪə	dear
æ	had	ɜː	bird	eə	chair
ɑː	car	ə	away	ʊə	sure
ɒ	dog	eɪ	pay		
ɔː	ball	aɪ	cry		

p	put	f	first	h	house
b	best	v	van	m	must
t	tell	θ	three	n	next
d	day	ð	this	ŋ	song
k	cat	s	sell	l	love
g	good	z	zoo	r	rest
tʃ	cheese	ʃ	ship	j	you
dʒ	just	ʒ	pleasure	w	will

(r) shows a linking r, pronounced before a vowel but (in British English) not before a consonant

ˈ precedes a stressed syllable

Other symbols

The symbol / (forward slash) between two words or phrases means that either is possible.

We also uses slashes around phonetic symbols, e.g. *tea* /tiː/.

Brackets ( ) around a word or phrase in an example mean it can be left out.

→ means that two things are related.

~ means that there is a change of speaker.

▼ is a reference to the Word Focus where there is more information.

Acknowledgements

The authors and publisher are grateful to those who have given permission to reproduce the following extracts and adaptations of copyright material:

p.84 James Yolkowski, 'Buildings, Structures, and Monuments Facts', www.allfunandgames.ca/facts/buildings.shtml. Reproduced by kind permission.

p.122 Extract from 'Togo terrorist attack is threat to the 2010 World Cup finals' by Ralph Ellis, 8 January 2010, *Daily Mail*. Reproduced by permission of Solo Syndication.

p.124 Extract from 'Dramatic pictures as motorbike gang raid The Queen's jewellers' by Jon Clements, 10 March 2010, www.mirror.co.uk. Reproduced by permission.

p.232 Extracts from 'How do I plan revision?' from www. napier.ac.uk. Reproduced by kind permission of Edinburgh Napier University.

p.236 Extracts adapted from 'MA Education - Programme' from www.bath.ac.uk. Reproduced by kind permission of the University of Bath.

p.252 Extracts from 'Dos and don'ts' from www.ucas.com. Reproduced with kind permission of UCAS: www.ucas.com.

p.282 Extracts from 'The Marketing Secret Widely Known but Rarely Practiced' by Joel Sussman. Copyright 2011 Joel N. Sussman, Marketing Survival Kit.com. Reproduced by kind permission.

p.314 Public sector information licensed under the Open Government Licence v1.0.

Sources:

p.8 Source: www.mindbodylife.com.au
p.38 Source: www.bbc.co.uk
p.96 Source: adapted from 'Email etiquette' from www.emailreplies.com.
p.108 Source: www.wikipedia.com
p.278 Source: www.londonapprenticeship.co.uk
p.280 Source: www.iveybusinessjournal.com
p.284 Source: www.rolandberger.com

Authors' acknowledgements

We are greatly indebted to Julia Elliott for her expert advice on the manuscript, and also to Peter and Karen Viney.

Illustrations by:
Stefan Chabluk pp 6, 58, 162;
Paul Daviz p 334;
Mark Duffin pp 92, 94, 95, 96;
Karen Hiscock pp 128, 129, 130, 131, 132, 133;
Chris Pavely p 2;
Peters & Zabransky UK Ltd pp 154, 156, 157;
Peter Richardson pp 18, 138, 139, 152, 168;
Dan Svatek/+ Colagene Illustration Clinic pp 214, 215, 216, 217;

We would also like to thank the following for permission to reproduce photographs:

Alamy Images pp 46 (Couple with dog/Roger Lee), 64

ACKNOWLEDGEMENTS

(Medicine/ImageDJ), 80 (Rhinoceros/M & J Bloomfield), 80 (Giant Panda/Life on white), 90 (Brick wall/photogen), 90 (Brick/Mode Images Limited), 124 (Broken shop window/Corbis Bridge), 134 (Slices of liver/Foodcollection.com), 134 (Pheasant/Norman Price), 134 (Turkey/Prisma Bildagentur AG), 135 (Tuna steak/Keith Leighton), 135 (Carp/Universal Images Group Limited), 135 (Crayfish/Alex Generay), 135 (Cockle shells/Art Directors & TRIP), 141 (Chicken drumsticks/foodfolio), 146 (Fruit stall/Robin Chapman), 151 (Cardigan/Art Directors & TRIP), 151 (Bikini/D.Hurst), 178 (Hikers/Aurora Photos), 190 (Car passenger ferry/David Lyons), 190 (Cargo ship/Ron Bedard), 268 (Bricklayer/Roger Bamber), 268 (Refuse collection/chrisstockphoto), 352 (Pensive woman/Corbis Flint); Bridgeman Art Library Ltd p 204 (Self Portrait, 1888 (oil on canvas), Gogh, Vincent van (1853-90) / Private Collection / Photo © Christie's Images); Corbis pp 26 (Woman relaxing outdoors/Oliver Rossi/Fancy), 116 (Chilean miner rescue/CEZARO DE LUCA/epa), 120 (Offshore oil well fire/HO/Reuters), 174 (Gardener/Darren Kemper), 190 (Family in rowing boat/Tony Arruza), 312 (Radio jockey/Hemant Mehta/India Picture), 352 (Surly teen male/Ocean), 352 (Female portrait/Kelly Redinger/Design Pics); Getty Images pp 78 (Chimpanzee/Geoff Dann), 79 (Common seal/Frank Greenaway), 79 (Swan/John Foxx), 79 (Penguin/Digital Zoo), 167 (Ladder/C Squared Studios); Hemera Technologies Inc. pp 64 (Bandage), 64 (Tweezers), 78 (Tiger), 78 (Polar bear), 79 (Dolphin), 79 (Crocodile), 80 (Tiger), 134 (Kidneys), 134 (Rabbit), 166 (Rusty Wrench), 210 (Cello), 210 (Brass trumpet); iStockphoto pp 151 (Waistcoat/Руслан Кудрин), 151 (Pyjamas/Peggy De Meue); Masterfile pp 151 (Nightgown/Glowimages), 190 (Fishing boat/Scanpix Creative); OUP p 24 (World Cup/UKraft), 36 (), 64 (Plasters/Gareth Boden), 66 (Brain scan/Photodisc), 74 (Polar bear/Photodisc), 74 (Alaska/Digital Vision), 78 (Camel/Photodisc), 78 (Giraffe/Ingram), 78 (Zebra/Ingram), 78 (Kangaroo/Photodisc), 78 (Wolf/Photodisc), 79 (Shark/Ingram), 79 (Eagle/Ingram), 79 (Owl/Photodisc), 79 (Macaw/Photodisc), 134 (Duck/Photodisc), 134 (Billy goat/Photodisc), 135 (Lobster/Photodisc), 135 (Steamed crab/Photodisc), 135 (Mussels/Melba Photo Agency), 135 (Pearl in oyster/Photodisc), 135 (Squid/Iconotec), 137 (Almonds/Stockbyte), 166 (Screw/Photodisc), 166 (Screwdriver/Dennis Kitchen Studio, Inc), 166 (Nails/Dennis Kitchen Studio, Inc), 166 (Nut and bolt/Ingram), 166 (Hammer/Ingram), 167 (Saw/Ingram), 167 (Electric drill/Melba Photo Agency), 167 (Paint tin and brush/Ingram), 167 (Paint roller and tray/Ingram), 190 (Cruise ship/David R. Frazier Photolibrary, Inc.), 190 (Sailing boat/Ingram), 190 (Canoeing/Creatas), 220 (Trophy cup/Photodisc); Photolibrary pp78 (Silverback Gorilla/Stockbrokerxtra Images), 86 (Lucknam Park Hotel/Britain On View); Science Photo Library p 66 (MRI scan// pasieka).